RELIGIOUS STUDIES COURSE
FOR GCSE

Jesus in the Synoptic Gospels

by

DIANA MORGAN

EDITORIAL ADVISER: EDWIN COX

Emeritus Reader in Education University of London

ISBN 0 264 67111 2 (*trade edition*)
ISBN 0 264 67031 0 (*schools edition*)

First published 1987
by A.R. Mowbray & Co. Ltd,
Saint Thomas House, Becket Street,
Oxford, OX1 1SJ

Phototypeset by Getset (BTS) Ltd, Eynsham, Oxford
Printed in Great Britain by Bell and Bain Ltd., Glasgow

British Library Cataloguing in Publication Data

Morgan, Diana, 1931-
Jesus in the Synoptic Gospels.
1. Jesus Christ
I. Title
232 BT202

ISBN 0-264-67111-2
ISBN 0-264-67031-0 non-net

MOWBRAY LONDON & OXFORD

CONTENTS

PREFACE FOR TEACHERS

This course is designed to meet the needs of the new General Certificate of Secondary Education (GCSE) which calls for a fresh approach to familiar material.

The book is suitable for use with the syllabuses of the principal examining boards. St Mark's Gospel forms the basis of the study but cross references are given to the other Synoptic Gospels. In addition the Q passages and stories special to Luke and Matthew are included when they form part of the syllabuses.

The national criteria require the examination to assess the candidates' ability in the following areas:

1. Selection and presentation of factual information.
2. Understanding of a variety of religious concepts and responses.
3. Evaluation of issues of belief and practice.

Therefore the questions provided in each unit cover these three areas.

The course is planned with mixed ability teaching in mind. There is ample material to keep academic pupils stretched yet the style of presentation is designed to appeal to all levels of ability. It is left to the individual teacher's experience to decide which students need to spend their time absorbing factual information and which are ready to proceed to the more demanding tasks of evaluation. The variety of questions makes it possible for all members of a class to be working on a single topic yet at different levels.

To make this possible, presentation has been simplified as follows:

1. The main text contains the basic factual information necessary for all candidates following the course.
2. Background information, which need not be slavishly learned for the examination but which will help bring the gospels to life, is given in the tinted panels.
3. Boxed areas marked ● contain information necessary for the more demanding levels of understanding and are essential for those making an academic approach to the subject.

Are you ready? . . . Get set! . . .

The units can, of course, be studied in any order. Each unit represents approximately one week's work but the length of time spent will naturally vary from class to class. Students will need to have a copy of the gospels and to familiarise themselves with the names given to events, parables and miracles according to the version of the Bible specified in their particular syllabus.

Illustrations are designed to link the gospel narrative to the twentieth century. By the time students have reached the fourth year of secondary education, most of them are familiar with biblical costume and customs and are more interested in finding answers to questions concerning the relevance of the gospels to life in our own day. It is hoped that the course will help them in their search.

How can we know Jesus existed?

How do you know William the Conqueror existed? Well — how *do* you know? Try to work it out for yourself. Think. Here are some possible reasons:

1. Documents and artefacts exist from the time, for example, the Bayeux Tapestry.
2. There is plenty of cultural evidence even today of the Norman invasion which changed our history and way of life. For example our language is full of words of French origin (we speak of pigs, but they become pork when cooked, as sheep become mutton.)

Similar kinds of evidence are available for the life of Jesus. Historical evidence needs to be as near in time as possible to the events being described. It is difficult to publish lies if there are people still alive who can contradict you. Books published about the Second World War at the present time are likely to be substantially correct in fact, although interpretations of events may be open to question. There are still plenty of people alive who would write angry letters to *The Times* if an author wrote a travesty of the truth.

So what documentary evidence have we, written within a reasonable time of Jesus himself, which compares with the kind of evidence we have for the existence of William the Conqueror?

1. EVIDENCE FROM DOCUMENTS

(a) DOCUMENTS FROM NON-CHRISTIAN SOURCES

If people are not interested in promoting the cause of Jesus and yet mention him in their writing, even in passing, this is very good evidence that he must have existed.

> **TEST YOURSELF ON FACTS**
> 1. What were the names of the three Romans who refer to Jesus in their writings?
> 2. What is the name of the Jewish historian who wrote the Jewish Antiquities?
> 3. How many books are there in the New Testament?
> 4. What is the name of the book which gives an account of the growth of Christianity up to AD 62?

Three historians of the time write of Jesus and a fourth mentions the troublesome Christians.

(i) **Tacitus**, a Roman historian, gives an account of the burning of Rome in AD 64 for which Christians were blamed. In his *Annals* Tacitus tells us that the Christians' leader had been executed on the order of Pontius Pilate during the reign of Tiberius. Tacitus was no friend of Christians but mentions the crucifixion, which bears out the gospel story.

(ii) **Suetonius**, writing in the first century AD, refers to a disturbance in Rome which took place in the reign of the Emperor Claudius and which resulted in the Emperor expelling troublemakers who followed 'Chrestus' — presumably a reference to Christians.

(iii) **Josephus**, a Jewish historian, wrote a book called *Antiquities of the Jews* in which he refers to Annas, Caiaphas, Pilate, John the Baptist and Jesus himself, referring to his death and resurrection and saying that, even at the time of writing, the tribe of Christians had not yet died out.

(iv) **Pliny**, a Roman administrator in what we call Turkey, wrote to the Emperor Trajan at the beginning of the second century asking what to do with the troublesome Christians. Trajan replied that he should persuade them to give up their belief but need not persecute them.

Does it seem likely that people would be prepared to suffer and even go to their death for a leader who never existed?

(b) DOCUMENTS FROM CHRISTIAN SOURCES

The evidence about Jesus from Christian writers is contained in the twenty-seven books of the New Testament (the word 'testament' means 'covenant/agreement').

(i) First in time come **twenty-one letters**. One of these (1 Cor. 15.3–8) contains the earliest reference to the resurrection and it was written within twenty years of the event itself.

(ii) Secondly there are the **Four Gospels** (the word 'gospel' means 'good news'). When the last eyewitnesses were coming to the end of their lives, they thought it necessary to make a written record. Previously stories about Jesus had been passed on by word of mouth. It was a 'preached message' — *kerygma* in Greek.

A Billy Graham rally at Sheffield in 1985. It is even more likely in the twentieth century than it was in the first century that people who have been impressed by a preached message will turn to the written word to learn more.

- ***THE KERYGMA COULD BE SUMMARISED AS FOLLOWS:***

Old Testament prophecies have been fulfilled;
The Messiah, descended from King David, has been born. He is Jesus of Nazareth who spent his life teaching and healing.
He was crucified in order to fulfil God's will;
He came to life three days later and now has the place of honour in heaven;
He will come again in glory to judge us;
Therefore repent and be baptized.

(iii) Thirdly we have the **Acts of the Apostles**, which gives an account of the growth of Christianity up to AD 62.

(iv) Fourthly, there is the book of **Revelation**, a special kind of writing, which need not concern us here.

CHECK YOUR UNDERSTANDING

1. *What does the word 'testament' mean?*
2. *What does the word 'gospel' mean?*
3. *What does the word '**kerygma**' mean?*
4. *Can you summarise the **kerygma**?*

These books form the written evidence of Jesus' friends and supporters.

2. THE EXISTENCE OF THE CHRISTIAN CHURCH

Since the Christian Church has existed for two thousand years and there are now estimated to be 1433 million Christians in the world, something must have happened to start it. Nearly forty per cent of the world's population today worship Jesus as God. An anonymous author has put it like this: 'I am well within the mark when I say that all the armies that ever marched, and all the parliaments that ever sat, and all the kings that ever reigned, put together, have not affected the life of man upon earth as has this one solitary life.'

WHAT DO YOU THINK?

1. Would you prefer the evidence of Christians or non-Christians in forming your own view of Jesus? Why?
2. How would you assess the truth or otherwise of a new religion? Look up Acts 5.34–39 to see how Gamaliel, a wise rabbi, approached the problem.

Authorship, purpose and characteristics of the Synoptic Gospels

There are Four Gospels but three of them, Matthew, Mark and Luke, are so similar in approach that we call them the Synoptic Gospels (Greek *syn* = together + *opsis* = viewing) i.e. they are written from the same point of view. The Fourth Gospel, which bears the name of John, is totally different in style and does not form part of your syllabus.
What was the purpose of the synoptic writers? What do we know about them? In what ways do they differ from each other?

1. PURPOSE

The purpose of the writers was to lead people to share their own faith that Jesus was the Christ, the Son of God and they told stories which would demonstrate this belief. So the gospels are a record of what Christians *believed* about Jesus, *not* biographies. The writers were, in fact, recording the *kerygma* (Introduction 1 (b)(ii)), following up the preached message.

2. THE WRITERS

It may come as a surprise to realise that it is unlikely that any of the synoptic writers was numbered among the twelve apostles, nor were they necessarily present at the events they describe. Scholars are divided as to precisely when the gospels were written although all are agreed that St Mark's must have been the first.

(a) ST MARK*

(i) **The Man**

From earliest times he has been identified with Mark whose name occurs quite frequently in the early history of the Church. An early tradition makes a very close link between St Mark and St Peter so that St Mark's Gospel is often regarded as Peter's memories of the life of Jesus, although it is a sophisticated piece of writing not just a jumble of an old man's memories.

There is one personal touch in this Gospel. In his account of the arrest of Jesus he tells us: 'Among

St Mark is specially honoured in Venice

those following was a young man with nothing on but a linen cloth. They tried to seize him, but he slipped out of the linen cloth and ran away naked.' (Mark 14.51 NEB). This young man was probably Mark and his words were his way of saying 'I was there and saw it for myself.'
Later Mark met St Paul and went on his first missionary journey. These links with both St Peter and St Paul are important. They show Mark to be close to reliable sources.

(ii) **Reasons for writing**

Christians were blamed for the fire in Rome during the reign of Nero. (Introduction 1 (a) (i)). Not many of them had friends in high places; strange rumours existed about them such as that they were cannibals, eating 'flesh' and drinking 'blood' at a secret meal they shared together. Furthermore they were refusing to burn incense to honour the Emperor as a god. They were ripe for liquidation. Both Peter and Paul were executed and so Mark wrote his Gospel to encourage Christians to cling to their faith in those terrible times.

> • *EVIDENCE*
>
> *Bishop Papias, writing in the second century, records the evidence of an elder thus: 'This also the Presbyter used to say: Mark indeed, who became the interpreter of Peter, wrote accurately as far as he remembered them the things said or done by the Lord, but not however in order.'*
> *— quoted in the version used by Rawlinson, Westminster Commentary p. xxv — Methuen*

* *SYMBOLS OF THE EVANGELISTS. The symbols of the evangelists are derived from a vision in the Book of Revelation (4.7). Among the many interpretations are the following: St Mark is symbolised by the lion roaring in the wilderness 'Prepare ye the way of the Lord'.* (Look up the opening of his gospel). *St Luke, who begins his gospel with a priest in the Temple, is symbolised by a winged ox, a sacrificial animal. St Matthew begins his gospel with Christ's human ancestry, so his symbol is a man with wings of spiritual power.*

(iii) **Characteristics of St Mark's Gospel**

Vigour

The Gospel has a vigorous, almost breathless style. The word 'immediately' (Greek *euthus*) occurs forty-one times. The drama moves at a tremendous pace.

Personal

The writing is vivid and St Peter's personal memories seem very close: 'Go and give this message to his disciples *and Peter* . . .' says the angel at the empty tomb.

Humanity

Jesus is portrayed as fully human. He is moved with pity at the sight of suffering; he snorts with anger; grows indignant with his misguided disciples; warms to the rich young man seeking eternal life and is seized by a shuddering fear as he faces up to the crucifixion in the Garden of Gethsemane.

Authority

Yet there is no doubt in Mark's mind that Jesus is *more* than human. He speaks with authority; even the winds and the waves obey him. He speaks of his own death as 'the blood of the covenant shed for many.'

(b) ST LUKE*

(i) **The Man**

In St Luke we meet an educated man, a doctor who joined St Paul at the port of Troas on his second missionary journey. Possibly Paul was ill and in need of his professional help. Later Paul was to refer to him as 'dear Dr Luke.' (Col. 4.14).

Paul and Luke crossed the sea together to Europe and Luke's first experience of Paul's missionary activity would have been in Philippi.

It is generally agreed that St Luke must have been a Gentile (Col. 4.11 – 14) but one who was familiar with the Greek Old Testament. In his Gospel he shows constant interest in Gentiles and, having been a slave, retains a warm sympathy for the outcasts of society. His medical training is reflected in his use of technical medical terms in his Gospel.

> MEDICINE IN THE TIME OF CHRIST
>
> **Doctors in ancient times were not accorded the social status they enjoy today. Many were slaves who were bought by the wealthy and kept for the exclusive use of their own households. Medical knowledge was largely a matter of herbal remedies but operations could be performed, though of course without anaesthetics. We know, for example, that tracheotomy (cutting into the windpipe) was carried out.**

**See footnote on page 5*

(ii) **Reasons for writing**

In the prologue to his Gospel St Luke tells us that he knows others have already told the story but says he has decided to give an account which will give 'authentic knowledge about the matters of which you have been informed.' (NEB) He emphasises that he has checked the information of eyewitnesses.

(iii) **Characteristics of St Luke's Gospel**

Gentile emphasis

Luke writes for educated Gentiles showing them that Jesus was for everyone and, although he was the expected Jewish Messiah, his ministry was not confined to the Jews.

Scholarly

Luke was a skilled writer who could vary his style to suit his narrative. The characters he describes come vividly alive and *the student is well advised to make a conscious effort to remember which stories are parables and which are events which actually took place. It is easy to become confused when the narrative is so alive.*

Anti-racist

St Luke is consistently anti-racist. We owe our record of the parable of the Good Samaritan to him. Samaritans were despised by the Jews and part of the power of that story lies in the racial origin of its hero.

Sympathy

Having been a slave himself, he has great sympathy for the underdog and for those despised by religious people. 'The Son of Man came to seek and to save the lost,' he tells us (Luke 19.10) and shows how Jesus consistently, throughout his life, made friends with tax collectors, lepers and the outcasts of society.

Understanding

St Luke shows an understanding and sympathy for women unusual at the time. For instance, in the story of the raising to life of the son of the widow of Nain, Jesus' concern is focused on the widow rather than her son — 'the only son of his mother

TEST YOURSELF ON FACTS

1. Which are the Synoptic Gospels?
2. Which was the first Gospel to be written?
3. With which two apostles was St Mark associated? On whose memories is his Gospel based?
4. What was Mark doing in Rome when Nero persecuted the Christians?
5. Which Gospel is regarded as the most accurate?
6. Which of the gospel writers uses most quotations from the Old Testament?

and she was a widow . . . he had compassion on her . . . he gave him to his mother.'

Prayer

Luke, more than the other writers, shows us the importance of prayer in the life of Jesus. For example he alone tells us that Jesus was praying at the time of his baptism and that he prayed all night before choosing his twelve disciples.

(c) ST MATTHEW*

(i) **The Man**

It is unlikely that Matthew the disciple of Jesus wrote the Gospel which bears his name. In Unit 2 we shall see that he copies heavily from St Mark — 606 of St Mark's 661 verses reappear in St Matthew. If the writer had known Jesus personally surely he would have written his own book rather than basing his work on St Mark.

Yet it is probable that there is a connection between the two Matthews. Scholars believe there must have existed a collection of Jesus' sayings in Hebrew which the disciple Matthew probably made (known as Q — see Unit 2). These were used by Christian teachers in whatever ways they wished and both Matthew and Luke draw freely from Q in their gospels. We know little about the writer of the Gospel personally apart from what we can deduce from his book. He must have been a Jewish Christian, perhaps a converted rabbi.

(ii) **Reasons for writing**

Matthew is writing primarily for Jewish Christians to strengthen their faith that Jesus is the Messiah. The particular Christian community he was serving was probably in Syrian Antioch and the likely date of writing is in the eighties of the first century.

(iii) **Characteristics of St Matthew's Gospel**

Recourse to the Old Testament

This Gospel makes frequent reference to the Old Testament. Sometimes the Evangelist uses direct quotation ('this took place to fulfil what the Lord had spoken by the prophet. . . .'); many more times he echoes Old Testament phrases.

Importance of the Church

For St Matthew the Church is central to the work of Christ. He alone records Jesus saying 'You are Peter, the rock, and on this rock I will build my Church' (16.18 NEB). The final words of the Gospel are 'And be assured, I am with you always to the end of time.' In other words, it is the Church which is to continue Christ's work in the world.

Colourful details

Although Matthew relies heavily on St Mark's Gospel, he seems to make additions of a miraculous nature (e.g. an earthquake before the women come to the tomb on Easter morning) and, because of this, it is the least reliable gospel from an historical point of view.

End of world expectancy

Like the other gospel writers, Matthew expected the world to end in the immediate future and this idea is most clearly expressed in his Gospel (see Chapter 24 and the parables in chapter 25).

Instruction for Christians

To help the members of the Church lead a Christ-centred life, Matthew records five great discourses (chapters 5–7: chapter 10: chapter 13: chapter 18: chapters 23–25) which together provide instruction for living the Christian life. The most famous of these discourses is the Sermon on the Mount (chapters 5–7).

CHECK YOUR UNDERSTANDING

1. *What does the word 'synoptic' mean?*
2. *What does the word 'evangelist' mean?*
3. *What is the theme of all the gospels?*
4. *What are the differences between a gospel and a biography?*
5. *Why was it easy to make Christians scapegoats for the fire in Rome in the reign of Nero?*
6. *In what ways can we see the influence of St Luke's own personal experience in his Gospel?*
7. *Until recently St Matthew's Gospel was the one most frequently used by the Church. Can you suggest reasons?*
8. *Delete whichever does not apply:*
   Mark was writing mainly for Jews/Gentiles/Romans
   Luke was writing mainly for Jews/Gentiles/Greeks
   Matthew was writing mainly for Jews/Gentiles/Christians

WHAT DO YOU THINK?

1. Does it matter that the writers of the Synoptic gospels were not numbered among the twelve apostles? Give reasons for your opinion.
2. What kind of knowledge do the gospels bring if they are not biographies?

**See footnote on page 5*

Synoptic problem: relationship between the Gospels

In Unit 1 we hinted at connections between the three synoptic gospels and must now come to grips with this topic. You will need to have some acquaintance with what is meant by the terms source criticism, form criticism and redaction criticism.

1. SOURCE CRITICISM

Where did the gospel writers find the material for their gospels? This in a nutshell is what source criticism is all about and a study of sources rapidly leads to what is known as the Synoptic Problem.

(a) THE USE OF ST MARK'S GOSPEL

When the three synoptic gospels are examined side by side the agreement between them goes far beyond what one would expect from the fact that they are all writing about the same person, Christ. Even the theory that all three writers were using the *kerygma* is insufficient to account for the close verbal similarities between the gospels. Matthew contains nearly all of Mark's Gospel and Luke contains just over half of it and both Matthew and Luke reproduce Mark's wording in a way which would quickly lead to copyright claims in our own day.

The first deduction we can make from source criticism therefore is that **St Mark's Gospel was the first to be written and was used by both Luke and Matthew in writing their own.**

(b) Q

If we look at the material which is common to Matthew and Luke but which does not appear in Mark, we find it consists of sayings of Jesus. Since Matthew and Luke were writing independently of each other they must have had access to another document. This document has never been found but we know from Papias (p.5) that a collection of Jesus' teaching existed, that it was in Aramaic (the language which Jesus spoke) and that it was translated by people as they wished. Scholars have called this document 'Q' (from the German word *Quelle* = 'source'). By comparing the passages in Matthew and Luke which are similar it is possible to reconstruct at least part of Q and it seems to have consisted of advice for new Christians on how to live the Christian life.

The second deduction we can make from source criticism is that **both Matthew and Luke had access to Q, which was not used by Mark.**

(c) M

Nonetheless Matthew's Gospel still contains some 300 verses of material not found elsewhere. These are known as 'Special Matthew' or 'M'. We do not know the source of this material but it is Jewish in tone. Some of it consists of the Old Testament prophecies already mentioned in Unit 1 (p.7). It also includes stories about the birth of Jesus which appear nowhere else.

The third deduction to be made from source criticism is that **St Matthew's Gospel is made up of three strands which can be expressed thus:**

Matt. = Mark + Q + M

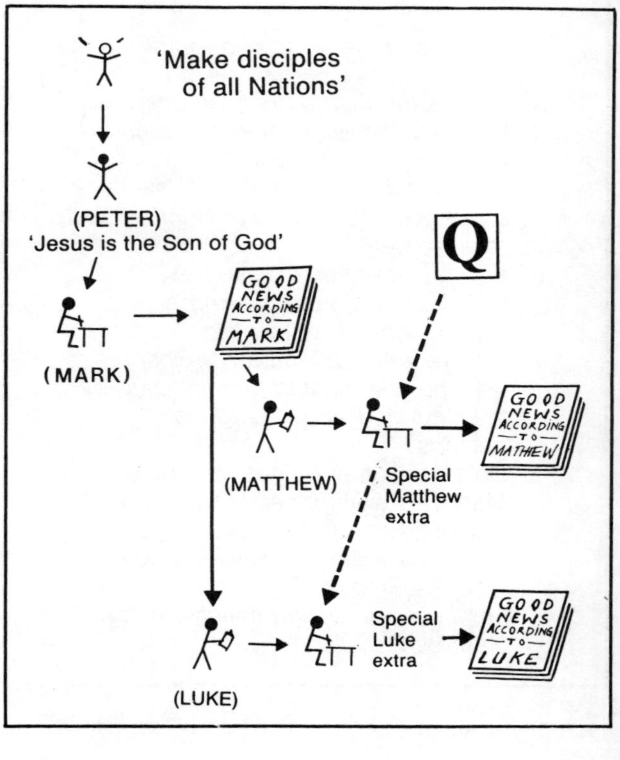

(d) L

Similarly much material in Luke is independent of Mark and Q and is known as 'L' or 'Special Luke'. This includes stories of the birth of Jesus, which clearly come from a source quite different from Matthew's, and some of the best known parables (the Good Samaritan, the Prodigal Son).

A fourth deduction we can make from source criticism is that **St Luke's Gospel is made up of three strands which can be expressed thus:**

Luke = Mark + Q + L

So in the Synoptic Gospels as a whole there are four strands — Mark, Q, L and M. It might help to learn this silly but useful rhyme:

Mark came first and so must be
Root and source of gospels three.
Luke and Matthew both used Q
Plus L or M — their special view.

2. FORM CRITICISM

In the early years of this century German scholars made an attempt to reach behind the written gospels to the traditions which had been handed down before the evangelists started writing. They believed that the stories in the gospels had existed as separate units and thought if they could cut through the editorial work of the gospel writers to the units themselves (*pericopes* is the technical word), they would come closer to the real Jesus. They therefore divided the gospel narrative into different types of stories such as parables, miracles, 'pronouncement' stories (i.e. stories which ended with a memorable pronouncement by Jesus which would stick in the listeners' minds) the stories like the baptism and transfiguration which were concerned with God revealing himself in a special way.

Through form criticism we come to see that the stories of Jesus had been shaped during the thirty years of oral tradition before the first gospel was written and that the task of the gospel writers was to weave existing material into continuous narrative.

TEST YOURSELF ON FACTS

1. What sources did St Luke use in writing his Gospel?
2. What do we mean by Q?
3. Which gospel writers used Q?
4. Give an example of material known as M.
5. Give an example of material known as L.

CHECK YOUR UNDERSTANDING

1. *What leads us to think there must have been a missing document which we call Q?*
2. *What is the aim of form criticism?*
3. *What do you understand by the word pericope?*
4. *What is the aim of redaction criticism?*

3. REDACTION CRITICISM

The most recent kind of criticism to be applied to the gospels is known as redaction criticism (redaction = editing). A simple way to understand its purpose is to imagine the gospel stories as colourful beads from which each evangelist selected those he wanted in order to create the particular pattern he had in mind. The interests of the individual writers have already been explained in Unit 1.

Redaction criticism helps us to understand that, right from the beginning, the evangelists were interpreters and not just recorders of the life and teaching of Jesus.

It is a blinkered view to regard the gospels as simple books of Bible stories. They are exciting and sophisticated writings which we are now ready to examine in an adult way.

WHAT DO YOU THINK?

1. Is it possible for a writer to describe (a) events (b) people, without allowing personal views to influence the description? How did Matthew, Mark and Luke allow their views to influence the gospels?
2. Should the Bible, which Christians believe to be the word of God, be subjected to the same kinds of criticism as any other literature? Give reasons for your answer.
3. Imagine you are appointed public relations manager for any contemporary personality you choose. How would you set about promoting him/her?

Luke Chapter 1

Before embarking on a study of the stories of the birth of Jesus, the student should take to heart one very imporant piece of advice:

STUDY THE TEXT

You will be examined on what is contained in the first two chapters of the gospels of St Luke and St Matthew and you must not confuse one gospel with the other. Nor should you introduce any of the legendary characters (such as the innkeeper and his wife) who have found their way into the story over the centuries. You are now to make an academic study for an examination and must pay careful attention to detail, avoiding flights of imaginative conversation and sticking as closely as possible to the text.

In each section you should begin by reading the passage concerned in whichever version of the Bible is specified in your syllabus and then study the notes. Remember that the examination is designed to show how well you understand the gospels and that it is on the **gospels** that you will be tested.

The early part of this Gospel has many mysterious happenings — angelic announcements, babies conceived in miraculous fashion, a young mother giving birth to her son in a stable, shepherds having a vision of angels — but for the purpose of the examination our concern must be to study the text as it stands.

1. FORETELLING OF THE BIRTH OF JOHN THE BAPTIST Luke 1.5–25

St Luke begins his Gospel not, as one might expect, with Jesus but with the foretelling of the birth of John the Baptist. The Jews expected that, before their long-awaited Messiah came (Messiah = anointed one i.e. specially chosen — a concept to be studied in more detail in Unit 5), God would send a forerunner to warn them so that they could prepare for his coming. John the Baptist was to be that forerunner.

Incense is still used in many churches and is burnt in a thurible rather like this.

v.5 Priests were grouped into twenty-four divisions, each division taking a turn of duty at the Temple in Jerusalem twice a year for a week at a time. The most coveted of the priestly duties was the burning of incense before the Holy of Holies at the morning and evening sacrifices.

> ● ***ANGELS***
>
> *St Luke mentions angels fourteen times. What are we to make of these heavenly beings? Angels form part of the poetic, symbolic language of the Bible in which the evangelists express their belief that God communicates with Man. They are messengers sent from God to influence human lives. As H.J. Richards has said, 'We do not know what they are, only what they mean.' To the gospel writers they meant 'the majesty and the transcendence, the protection and the revelation of God.'* The First Christmas: what really happened. *(Mowbray)*

v.9 Incense is made from a mixture of gums and fragrant spices. The smoke symbolises the prayers of the people rising to God.

It was for this duty that lots were drawn. Once the lot had fallen to a particular priest, he was never again included in the draw and many priests must have died without ever having had the experience. It was therefore the highlight of Zechariah's life when the lot fell to him. Lots were drawn immediately before the appointed time so that every priest went to the Temple carefully prepared in case the duty fell to him.

In our own day a last minute choice is made in King's College chapel, Cambridge on Christmas Eve. The famous carol service, broadcast each year, begins with a chorister singing the first verse of 'Once in royal David's city' solo. None of the choristers knows until the moment of going on the air which one of them will be called to sing that solo. What effect would this have on the preparation made by all the choristers? What effect might it have on the singing of the chosen boy if he knew in advance?

On such a momentous occasion Zechariah would have gone forward in a state of heightened awareness, taking with him the prayers of the people but also inevitably with personal prayers about his own childlessness. Zechariah and his wife would have suffered from the stigma which came from the common belief that not having children was a punishment from God for sin. Zechariah's wife, Elizabeth, was now past the age of childbearing and these two good people (v.6) were resigned to their lot but saddened by it. It is against this background that Zechariah had his vision of the angel Gabriel.

> **• *THE VIRGIN BIRTH***
>
> *The Christian doctrine of the Virgin Birth (i.e. that Jesus was born of a girl without sexual experience) can be approached in broadly one of two ways:*
> *1. As a straightforward historical account which need not be questioned since the Creator, who is alive and creating still, could act in this way.*
> *There are many, even among doubters, who find it easier to believe that God intervened in world history in a miraculous way than to accept that the world was changed by the wholly human child of two humble peasants living in a small town in first century Palestine.*
> *2. As a legend which has grown up as a way of explaining the Christian faith that God became man in Jesus. It is important to be quite clear, whichever view is taken, that the gospel writers are making a theological point rather than a biological one.*
> **Christian faith is that God became man in Jesus. That is what the doctrine of the Virgin Birth is all about.**

Notice in detail how St Luke records the message:

(a) Do not be afraid (so Zechariah must have been frightened)
(b) God has heard your prayer (so he must have been praying)
(c) Your wife will bear you a son (a miracle at Elizabeth's age).
(d) God then names the child. The name John means 'God is gracious' showing God has chosen this child for some special purpose even before he was born.

Notice how that purpose is set out in verses 15–17.

(e) The reference to not drinking wine fore-shadows John the Baptist taking the vows of a strict religious sect called the Nazirites who refrained from taking alcohol.
(f) The words in v.17 are based on the prophet Malachi (3.1 and 4.5) who said that Elijah, the great Old Testament prophet would return to this world before the day of the Lord to warn the people and prepare them for the coming of the Messiah. John the Baptist was to fulfil the spiritual role of Elijah.

Despite his awe in the presence of God's messenger, Zechariah argues. It seemed beyond belief that he and his wife should become parents at their age. He asks for proof and is given a punitive sign. He is struck dumb.

2. THE ANNUNCIATION Luke 1.26–37

Be very careful not to invent imaginative, colourful details. We are not told that Mary was performing any of the numerous housewifely tasks which examination candidates have suggested over the years.

Mary would have been a young girl — no older than the majority of students at school taking this examination — when she too was visited by the angel Gabriel. Notice the contrast with the visit to Zechariah. The angel's tone is more respectful — almost as though he were in the presence of a superior. Yet Mary is also fearful and needs reassurance.

Whereas the role of Zechariah's child was to go ahead of the Lord and prepare the people for the Lord's coming, Mary's child would be king of Israel forever and his kingdom would be eternal. Mary's question in verse 34 and the angel's reply raise the topic of the Virgin Birth and her acceptance of God's will in verse 38 marks an important turning point. The Gospel is saying that, had she not been prepared to co-operate, God would not have forced the issue i.e. that the birth of Christ depended on human co-operation.

Mary must have had great courage being prepared to face, at best, the loss of the love of the man to whom she was engaged when he found out that she was pregnant; at worst, she was facing the possibility of being stoned to death, the punishment for adultery. But Mary said 'Yes' to God. To

> **TEST YOURSELF ON FACTS**
> 1. Who visited both Zechariah and Mary?
> 2. What message did he bring to (a) Zechariah (b) Mary?
> 3. What did Zechariah say?
> 4. What did Mary say?
> 5. Who does Mary go to visit?

CHECK YOUR UNDERSTANDING

1. *What does the word 'angel' mean?*
2. *In two columns list the similarities and the differences between the stories of the foretelling of the birth of John the Baptist and the annunciation to Mary.*
3. *What was the role of John the Baptist to be? — look at 1.15–17 and 1.76–77*
4. *Summarise the Magnificat.*
5. *Write out the Benedictus in your own words.*

Christians the importance of Mary's 'Yes' is that it made possible the incarnation — God taking human flesh (from the Latin *caro* = flesh).

3. THE VISITATION Luke 1.39–56

This story links the accounts of the births of John and Jesus. The unborn forerunner leaps in his mother's womb to greet the unborn one he was to herald. The Evangelist uses a normal biological fact to make a theological point. Throughout these chapters St Luke is stretching language to its limit in his attempt to convey spiritual experience. It is Luke, the poet, who is speaking and we need to respond in the way that we would to poetry, music, art.

The Magnificat v.46–55
The first of the canticles (= little songs). Its name comes from the first word in the Latin version of the text. It is a patchwork of Old Testament quotations in which God is praised for the help he gives to those who are faithful to him. Refer to the Song of Hannah (1 Sam. 2.1–10) where another mother thanks God for granting her a son. Notice that the Magnificat begins with individual concerns and widens out to praise God for his help to *all* his people.

(a) Mary praises God for his love and mercy shown to humble people who are faithful to him.
(b) God turns upsidedown Man's ideas of greatness:
   (i) Proud people full of their own schemes are scattered;
   (ii) Those who are humble are raised above those of high status;
   (iii) The hungry are fed and the rich are turned away (*does this mean only hunger for food?*)
   (iv) God remains faithful to the promises he made to Abraham and his descendants.

4. BIRTH OF JOHN THE BAPTIST Luke 1.57–80

There is joy at the birth of a son to Elizabeth. Circumcision of Jewish boys takes place on the eighth day after birth (v.59) and is combined with the naming of the child. What inconsistency can you see between v.62 and what happened in v.20?

The Benedictus v.68–79
The second canticle. Its name comes from the first word in the Latin version of the text. It is similar in style to the Magnificat but, whereas Mary's song begins from individual concerns and widens to include the whole nation, Zechariah's song starts with the personal intervention of God in the affairs of the nation and gradually narrows down to the new-born John the Baptist (v.76).

It is a hymn which proclaims the fulfilment of God's plan. Learn carefully what it says:
The imminent arrival of the Messiah is happening in accordance with
(a) the words of the prophets
(b) God's promises made to our forefathers
(c) the covenant made with Israel
(d) the promises made to Abraham
Notice carefully what the role of the forerunner is to be (v.76–79). He is to prepare the way for the saviour by showing the people that salvation is to be received in the forgiveness of sins. (Salvation = 'health/wholeness').

WHAT DO YOU THINK?
The doctrine of the Virgin Birth forms part of the Apostles' Creed. Why do you think it is regarded as being so important?

Luke Chapter 2

1. BIRTH OF JESUS Luke 2.1–20

(a) St Luke tells us that Jesus was born in Bethlehem. There had been a prophecy to this effect (Micah 5.2–5. See Prophecy 2 in Unit 5).

(b) The year of the birth of Jesus cannot be fixed precisely. Both Luke (3.1) and Matthew agree that he was born while Herod the Great was still alive. Herod died in 4 BC. The year 0 from which our calendar is derived was incorrectly fixed by a sixth century Roman monk called Dionysius Exiguus who, endearingly, is remembered because of his mistake. The most likely date for the birth of Jesus is 6 (–5) BC. St Luke goes to great trouble to fix the birth of Jesus at a particular time in history (2.1–2).

(c) *Learn the text accurately and in detail.*
(i) The Romans merely required a census (v.4). It was Jewish national feeling (which the Romans were prepared to tolerate in these circumstances) which required everyone to go to his native city.
(ii) Swaddling clothes (v.7) were strips of cloth which were bound round a baby's limbs in the belief that doing so would help them to grow straight.

In this story Christians emphasise that, right from the time of his birth, there was no room for the Christ they worship.

- ***PRESENTATION OF THE FIRST-BORN***

This ceremony is based on the teaching in Exod. 13.12 and Num. 18.16. Any time after the first month the first-born was to be presented to God in the Temple and 'redeemed' by the payment of five shekels. The ceremony acted as a reminder that the child comes from God and belongs to him and can never be the possession of his parents.

- ***PURIFICATION OF THE MOTHER***

This ceremony is derived from Lev. 12. A woman was regarded as ritually unclean for forty days after childbirth and was not allowed to join in public worship. Purification involved sacrificing a lamb and a turtledove, but the poor were allowed to substitute two pigeons, the offering made by Mary and Joseph. Luke appears to have telescoped or confused these two ceremonies which, of course, would not have been of great interest to his Gentile readers.

It is unlikely that St Luke had in mind our idealised Christmas card scene. Think of the reality.

(d) The news of the Messiah's birth is first given to shepherds. The words of the carol, 'While shepherds watched their flocks by night' will help you to remember the song of the angels but be careful with the last line, which is more accurately translated in v.14 of modern versions of the Bible. As with Zechariah and Mary, the angel's first words to the shepherds are 'Fear not', — so great is their awe in the presence of God's messengers.
v.11 The prophets had foretold that the Messiah would be a descendant of the great King David (the word 'Christ' is the Greek form of the Hebrew word 'Messiah'.)
Be careful to learn accurately what happened in vv.15–17 and do not add legendary elements to the story half-remembered from childhood nativity plays.

(e) Above all, remember the joy of the shepherds and angels — a joy which is to chime throughout this whole Gospel.

WHAT DO YOU THINK?
How do you think God communicates with people in the twentieth century? Are these ways different from those in which he communicated with people in the first century?

2. PRESENTATION IN THE TEMPLE

Luke 2.22–40

Following the circumcision of the child (the name 'Jesus' is the Greek form of the Hebrew name 'Joshua' = 'Saviour'), Mary and Joseph go to the Temple in Jerusalem to fulfil two other religious duties of the Jews — the presentation of the first-born and the purification of the mother. There they meet two old and devout people, Simeon and Anna, both of whom recognise the greatness of the tiny child in his mother's arms.

> **CANDLEMAS**
> **This occasion in the Temple is remembered in some churches at Candlemas (February 2nd) when candles are lit as a reminder that Christ is the Light of the world.**

(a) SIMEON

The third canticle, the *Nunc Dimittis* (from the first words of the Latin text) is spoken by old Simeon. He recognises the child as the Messiah, yet as more than just one who has come for the glory of the Jews. This child will also be 'a light to lighten the Gentiles' (v.32). This phrase comes from Isaiah 49.6, one of the great poems about the suffering servant of God.

(b) ANNA

Anna, like Simeon, recognises Jesus as a significant figure who will help many people to find meaning in life.

3. FINDING IN THE TEMPLE Luke 2.41–52

At the age of twelve Jewish boys become Bar Mitzvah (= son of the Law) and take on for themselves the religious duties of an adult Jew.

On the first family visit to Jerusalem for Passover after Jesus had attained this status he lingered among the group on the Temple terrace listening to the rabbis (= teachers) discussing points of the religious Law and did not notice the rest of the family leaving for home with a party of pilgrims from Galilee. Jesus at this time was learning like any other twelve-year-old and, when he found himself among the best of the Jewish teachers, seized enthusiastically on the opportunity to learn from them. His knowledge of God grew gradually but, as his reply to Mary's gentle rebuke shows, he had now reached the point of relating the Jewish idea of the fatherhood of God to himself.

v.49 does not necessarily mean that he yet saw himself as the Son of God in the sense in which Christians use the words to describe the second person of the Trinity.

CHECK YOUR UNDERSTANDING

1. *Explain what is meant by (a) the Presentation of the first-born and (b) the Purification of the mother.*
2. *Explain the significance of the Bar Mitzvah ceremony.*

TEST YOURSELF ON FACTS

1. In which town was Jesus born?
2. Who was (a):Augustus?
   (b) Quirinius?
3. What was the purpose of Mary and Joseph's going to Bethlehem?
4. What is a manger?
5. What are swaddling clothes?
6. What did the angels tell the shepherds?
7. What was Mary's reaction to the shepherds' visit?
8. What does Simeon say about
   (a) Jesus? (b) Mary?
9. Who else in the Temple saw Jesus? What did she say?
10. What festival did Jesus attend in Jerusalem with his parents when aged 12?
11. What is meant by Bar Mitzvah?

> **BAR MITZVAH**
> **This ceremony takes place in the synagogue. The corresponding ceremony for girls is called Bath Mitzvah. Preparation consists of several years of lessons in Hebrew with instruction in the teachings of the Jewish Law.**
> **On the Sabbath following the boy's thirteenth birthday, he reads from the scriptures in the synagogue and then is presented with his tallith (= prayer shawl) and his siddur (= prayer book). He will wear the tallith on many occasions during his life and will be buried in it when he dies. After the ceremony there is a huge family party and the new Bar Mitzvah (or Bath Mitzvah) receives presents galore.**

UNIT 5

Nativity Stories in St Matthew's Gospel: Matt. 1.18 – 2.23

Before reading St Matthew's account of the birth of Jesus, remind yourselves of the characteristics of his Gospel listed in Unit 2 (p.7). Remember particularly his use of the Old Testament and notice here that he uses five Old Testament quotations to reinforce his conviction that Jesus is the long-awaited Messiah. The other noticeable characteristic, the emphasis he gives to the Church, emerges in these stories in the sense of worship which pervades them.

1. JOSEPH Matt. 1.18–24

Whereas St Luke mostly records the events which a mother would remember, St Matthew concentrates a little more on Joseph's point of view. We are told of his reaction when he finds that Mary is pregnant. Reference should be made to what has already been said about the Virgin Birth in Unit 3 (p.11). St Matthew supports his reference to the Virgin Birth by quoting from an Old Testament prophecy which appears to predict such an event.

> **• *OLD TESTAMENT PROPHECY 1***
> ***Isaiah 7.14***
> *'Behold a virgin shall conceive, and bear a son, and shall call his name Immanuel' (AV)*
> *'Immanuel' means 'God with us'*
> *Isaiah was writing about events in the time in which he himself was living, 800 years before Christ. King Ahaz of Judah was to be given a sign about the safety of his own kingdom. He was told that a child would be born and that, before the child was weaned, the king's enemies would be defeated. The word which was translated 'virgin' simply means 'young woman'. The young woman was probably Isaiah's own wife so it is hardly surprising that he knew she was going to have a child. Do you think Matthew is justified in using this quotation as if it were predicting a supernatural birth of a future Messiah?*

2. WISE MEN FROM THE EAST Matt. 2.

(a) IN JERUSALEM 2.1–8

Be very careful to learn the story accurately and do not include legendary additions in your examination answers.

CAREFUL!
We are not told how many wise men there were.
We are not told the colour of their skin.
We are not told they were kings.
We are not told their names

(i) The wise men (magi) could have been astrologers and possibly from Babylon which was famous as a centre for studying the stars. In those days astrology was taken very seriously. The magi had connected the appearance of an unusually bright star with the well-known Jewish expectation of a Messiah.

(ii) The bright star might have been the effect of Jupiter crossing the paths of Venus and Saturn which happened in 7 BC but there is also symbolism here. For instance in the Old Testament (Num. 24.17) the coming of a king is described in the following terms:
'there shall come a star out of Jacob and a sceptre shall rise out of Israel.' (AV)

(iii) The wise men showed they were Gentiles when they asked for 'the king of the Jews' (v.2) Jews did not refer to themselves as 'Jews' but would have asked for the 'King of Israel'. So **the Magi represent the learned men of the wider world coming to worship the Messiah.**

(iv) Herod had become king in 37 BC and was allowed to continue to reign because he co-operated with the Romans. He was very unpopular with his people and feared someone might usurp his place. He was therefore constantly watchful and had no intention of allowing anyone else to claim the title of 'king'.

Christmas crib at Epiphany in St Barnabas church, Ealing, West London. Notice that the figures of the shepherds have been removed.

(b) IN BETHLEHEM Matt. 2.9–12

(i) The worship offered by the wise men is the beginning of the worship which is shown to Christ throughout this Gospel which, in turn, reflects the worship offered by the Church.

(ii) Notice in verse 11 that they went into the house — not the stable. Their journey had taken up to two years (v.16) and Jesus is now described as a child. The traditional Christmas crib scene with the wise men kneeling in the stable does not accurately reproduce the text.

(iii) They offer him three gifts symbolic of Christian beliefs about Jesus. The carol 'We three kings' is a useful reminder of these meanings.

Gold
Gold is a gift for kings (Ps.72.15), representing wealth and power. Christ is king.

Frankincense
Frankincense is made from a gum produced from a tree. It too is offered to kings but is also symbolic of priesthood, representing prayer and worship. Christ is priest.

Myrrh
Myrrh is a gum used in an ointment which was used for anointing kings (Ps. 45.8) but was also used for burial. The word 'Messiah' means 'Anointed one'. Christ would accomplish his work through suffering and death.

● ***OLD TESTAMENT PROPHECY 2***

Micah 5.2

'But thou, Bethlehem Ephratah, though thou be little among the thousands of Judah, yet out of thee shall he come forth unto me that is to be ruler in Israel.' (AV)

St Luke had clearly been familiar with this prophecy that the Messiah was to be born in Bethlehem but, as he was writing for Gentiles, did not quote it. St Matthew gives weight to the fulfilment of scripture.

3. THE FLIGHT INTO EGYPT Matt. 2.13–15

This part of the story is reminiscent of the Old Testament account of events in Egypt in the time before the Exodus when Moses had led the Israelites out of slavery to freedom. Matthew, being a Jewish Christian, found significance in pointing out similarities between this event in the life of Jesus and the earlier event in the life of the nation. As God had saved his chosen people then, so would he save Jesus now.

(a) Herod is about to kill Jewish children as the

● ***OLD TESTAMENT PROPHECY 3***

Hosea 11.1

'When Israel was a child, then I loved him, and called my son out of Egypt.' (AV)

Hosea is referring to God calling his chosen people out of Egypt at the time of the Exodus. Matthew turns the text into a prophecy.

EPIPHANY

The word 'Epiphany' literally means 'manifesting / showing'. The Western church celebrates the coming of the wise men at Epiphany (6 Jan), remembering that Christ was being shown to Gentiles. Eastern Orthodox Christians, on the other hand, are celebrating the Incarnation on that date.

This difference in the date for celebrating Christmas came about when Christianity spread out into the Gentile world. People in Egypt and Eastern countries celebrated the triumph of the sun over darkness on 6 January and it was natural for Christians in those lands to adapt the pagan festival to remind themselves of Jesus, 'the Light of the world', coming into a world of darkness. Christians in the West, however, celebrated the Incarnation to coincide with the time of the Saturnalia, a Roman festival in honour of the god Saturn.

The only thing of which we can be sure about the date of Jesus' birth is that it was *not* on 25 December.

Pharoah had once ordered the killing of all Israelite boy babies.

(b) Moses had been hidden by his mother and now Jesus is removed to a place of safety.

(c) Moses grew up to be the Saviour of his people and was the founder of the Old Covenant. Jesus too is to be the Saviour of his people and the founder of the New Covenant.

4. MASSACRE OF THE INNOCENTS

Matt. 2.16–18

We can see now why the angel had warned Joseph to take the holy family to a place of safety (2.13). Herod ruthlessly kills all the boys in the area who are two years old or younger in his determination to be rid of a rival king. St Matthew shows his belief that God had known in advance of this massacre by quoting the prophet Jeremiah.

> • ***OLD TESTAMENT PROPHECY 4***
>
> ***Jeremiah 31.15***
>
> *'A voice was heard in Ramah, lamentation, and bitter weeping; Rachel weeping for her children refused to be comforted for her children, because they were not.'*
>
> *Rachel had been the mother of Joseph and Benjamin. Their descendants (her 'children') were the children of Israel who, in the time of Jeremiah, were led away into exile in Babylon. Ramah was on the route they would have taken.*

5. RETURN TO ISRAEL

Following the death of Herod, Joseph is told to return to Israel but, because Archelaus, cruel Herod's cruel son, was now ruler in Jerusalem, Joseph takes Mary and Jesus to Nazareth in Galilee. Matthew again quotes 'what was spoken by the prophets.'

> • ***OLD TESTAMENT PROPHECY 5***
>
> *'He shall be called a Nazarene'.*
>
> *This prophecy is not in the Old Testament. Various suggestions have been made as to how the confusion arose. The suggestions explore a possible misunderstanding of words in the Hebrew language and need not concern us here.*

TEST YOURSELF ON FACTS

1. What did the angel say to Joseph when he was planning to break off his engagement to Mary?
2. In which town was Jesus born?
3. To which town did the wise men first come?
4. What question did they ask when they arrived?
5. What did Herod do then?
6. What instructions did Herod give the wise men?
7. How were they guided to the child?
8. What did they do when they saw Jesus?
9. What gifts did they offer him?
10. What instructions was Joseph then given by the angel?
11. What did Herod do when the wise men did not return?
12. Where did Joseph take Mary and the child when they returned from Egypt?

CHECK YOUR UNDERSTANDING

1. *What had Isaiah said which St Matthew interpreted as the foretelling of the virgin birth of Christ?*
2. *What does the word 'Immanuel' mean?*
3. *What meanings have been attached to the gifts brought by the wise men?*
4. *Which prophet had foretold Bethlehem as the place of the Messiah's birth?*
5. *What parallels can you see between the story of Moses and that of the birth of Jesus?*
6. *What elements in these two chapters do you find to be particularly characteristic of St Matthew's writing?*

WHAT DO YOU THINK?

Make a list of all the facts St Matthew tells us about the birth of Jesus and another list of all the facts St Luke tells us. Do the evangelists contradict each other? In what ways do their stories differ?

UNIT 6

Prologues to the Gospels. Proclamation of John the Baptist

1. PROLOGUES TO THE GOSPELS

A bearer of news must first attract the attention of an audience and make sure that they pay attention to the announcement. That is what the evangelists are doing in the prologues to their gospels.

(a) MARK 1.1

'This is the good news about Jesus Christ, the Son of God.' (GNB) St Mark states here in one sentence the same faith that St Matthew and St Luke were to express through their stories of the birth of Jesus (Units 3 and 4) i.e. that Jesus of Nazareth is the Messiah. This is the first time the word 'Christ' is applied to Jesus. The word 'Christ' is the Greek form of the Hebrew word 'Messiah' (= anointed one).

(b) MATTHEW 1.1 – 17 (compare Luke 3.23 – 38)

The great family tree which forms the prologue to St Matthew's Gospel is designed to show that Jesus was descended not only from King David, which would be important for Jews who expected the Messiah to be 'Son of David', but also to show Jesus' descent from Abraham. Abraham was the founding father of the nation. God had made a covenant with him (Gen. 12.1 – 3) in which he had promised that through Abraham all the nations of the earth would be blessed.

We do not need to study the family tree in detail. St Luke (3.23 – 38) also gives us a family tree (which does not altogether coincide with St Matthew's) but Luke, a Gentile, does not stop at Abraham. He takes the line back to Adam showing that the Messiah was for *all* men, not just the Jews.

(c) LUKE 1.1 – 4

The prologue to St Luke's Gospel is unlike the others. Furthermore it is a polished piece of writing such as one might expect from an educated, literary man.

The name 'Theophilus' means 'friend of God'. Various suggestions have been made as to his identity.

(i) The fact that Luke addresses him as 'Your Excellency' could mean that he was a high-ranking Roman official, using a pseudonym, who wanted to find out more about the new religion before committing himself to it — a sensible move in view of the persecution being suffered by Christians at the time.

Queen Elizabeth II at her coronation in Westminster Abbey. Our own kings and queens are anointed as a sign of consecration. The ceremony takes place before the Archbishop of Canterbury places the crown on the Sovereign's head.

(ii) He may have been the patron who had asked St Luke to write the Gospel.
(iii) It may just be addressed to any friend of God in every generation.

Notice how carefully St Luke lists his sources. He refers to
(i) the written records (v.1)
(ii) accounts of eyewitnesses (v.2)
(iii) his own studies (v.3)

● ***THE MESSIAH***

Kings and priests were anointed with oil when they took office i.e. they were 'anointed ones'. The Jewish expectation that God would send an 'anointed one' to save them develops steadily throughout the nation's troubled history.
The Messiah was given a number of titles:
1. ***Son of David***
A thousand years earlier, God had spoken to King David, the greatest King the Jews had ever known, through the prophet Nathan, saying 'Your family shall be established and your kingdom shall stand for all time in my sight, and your throne shall be established forever.' (2 Sam. 7.16 NEB*). Therefore many Jews expected that, when the Messiah came, he would be like King David, a royal leader, who would overthrow Israel's enemies and re-establish their worldly power.*
2. ***Son of Man***
*This title is derived from a vision recorded in the Book of Daniel. This book was written in order to encourage the people at a time when the Jews were being persecuted. The writer describes a number of visions showing that God would eventually restore his people. In one of them (Dan. 7.13) he wrote, 'behold one like the Son of man came with the clouds of heaven, and came to the Ancient of days, and they brought him near before him. And there was given him dominion, and glory, and a kingdom.' (*AV*)*
'The Ancient of days', of course, is the one eternal God. The Son of Man originally stood for the whole people of God but over the years the title came to refer to the Messiah whose kingdom would be everlasting.
Whichever title they favoured, Jews looked forward to the coming of the Messiah as the time when God would bring about his purpose, restore the Jewish nation and bring even the Gentiles to the knowledge of God.

2. PROCLAMATION OF JOHN THE BAPTIST

Mark 1.2 – 8: Matt. 3.1 – 12: Luke 3.1 – 18

At the time when the gospel opens, many Jews were on a tiptoe of expectation, waiting for the coming of the Messiah. St Mark's Gospel claims by quoting from the Old Testament prophets (Mal. 3.1 and Isa. 40.3) that this time has come.
Prophets were not people who looked into the future — like crystal gazers or palmists — but people who spoke out on behalf of God.
It was basic to the earliest preaching that the gospel

TEST YOURSELF ON FACTS
1. Who was the father of the Jewish nation named at the beginning of St Matthew's family tree of Jesus?
2. From which king did Jews expect the Messiah to be descended?
3. John the Baptist was doing the work expected of the Old Testament prophet . . . .
4. What clothing did John the Baptist wear?
5. John the Baptist fed on . . . . and . . . .

fulfilled what God had said in the past through his prophets.

John the Baptist began to preach beside the River Jordan and people went out to hear him. He was a striking 'hell-fire' type of preacher and, according to St Luke and St Matthew, not at all complimentary to those who went to hear him. He is here trying to shock people into taking notice, saying 'Either take notice of me and get ready, or face judgement unprepared when the Messiah comes.' He saw that too many of the Jews were content to rely on the fact that they were God's chosen people and so thought they were secure and would escape judgement. John was determined to show them that this was not good enough. God required of each individual an act of spiritual renewal. John was determined to arouse a response and the response he wanted appears in verse 4.

The word 'repent' (GNB 'turn away from your sins') is a very strong word in the original Greek — *metanoia*. It means completely to change your mind, to turn right round and face the other way, i.e. to face God. It is not just a question of feeling sorry for sins but of re-ordering life in obedience to God. Feelings have nothing to do with it — it is a matter of a determination to live life in accordance with God's will. The word 'sin' itself is used in the precise sense of doing things in defiance of the known will of God.

Following repentance of this kind, the people are to be baptised as a sign of the washing away of their sins and starting a new life.

CHRISTIAN BAPTISM ('Christening')
Baptism is the way in which Christians become members of the Church. The water which is poured over their heads (or, in some Churches, in which they are totally immersed) symbolises the forgiveness of all previous sins. In addition Christians believe three other things take place. These are expressed when the rest of the Christian family welcome the newly-baptised saying, in the words of the Alternative Service Book,

1. **We are members together of the body of Christ (i.e. living limbs in the body of people here to do Christ's work)**
2. **We are children of the same heavenly father (i.e. God has adopted them to be the brothers and sisters of his son, Jesus)**
3. **We are inheritors together of the kingdom of God (what is the difference between an heir and an inheritor?)**

Now look up the very last words of the Old Testament (Mal. 4.5). From these words the belief had grown that, before the Messiah came, the great prophet Elijah would return to warn the people to be prepared for his coming. Mark does not mention Elijah but in verse 6 the words in which John the Baptist is described recall the clothing of Elijah (2 Kings 1.8). His food too was that eaten by people who lived in the wilderness — locusts (which were eaten fried — and still are in some places) and the honey of wild bees.

Notice the contrast between John's baptism with water — the preparation — and the Messiah's expected baptism with the Holy Spirit — the power of God.

CHECK YOUR UNDERSTANDING

1. *What is the importance of the family trees in the gospels of St Matthew and St Luke?*
2. *Give two possible explanations of the identity of Theophilus.*
3. *What had led the Jews to expect the Messiah to be a royal and powerful person?*
4. *How would you deduce from the first four verses of his Gospel that St Luke was a careful historian?*
5. *What does the word 'prophet' mean?*
6. *What does the Greek word 'Metanoia' (= repentance) really mean?*
7. *Why are the similarities between John the Baptist and Elijah stressed by the Gospel writers?*
8. *What was the meaning of the baptism of John?*

WHAT DO YOU THINK?
Do you think John the Baptist's way of trying to frighten people into preparing for the coming of the Messiah is a good one? Give reasons. Discuss parallels in our own time of organisations which try to shock people into a response.

Baptism. Temptations

1. BAPTISM OF JESUS

Mark 1.9 – 11. Matt: 3.13 – 17: Luke 3.21 – 22

Before we look at the text we need to ask ourselves the question why Jesus, if he was, as Christians believe, without sin, should come to receive baptism at the hands of John.

The answer seems to lie in the fact that John was clearly doing God's work and so Jesus would wish to identify himself with what John was doing.

What happened?

St Luke (3.21) gives us an important clue when he tells us that Jesus was praying. The whole incident needs to be read with this fact clearly in mind. Something of supreme importance was happening in the mind of Jesus.

As he rose from the water *'he saw heaven opening'* (Mark 1.10) i.e. he was aware, as he prayed, of the close presence of God. *'the Spirit came down on him like a dove'* — Jesus was filled with the power of God's own spirit. Jews understood God's spirit to be like a dove. The same word was used in the book of Genesis when God's spirit brooded on the face of the waters of primeval chaos. So Jesus must have had some kind of vision through which he was aware of God's power coming to him.

And a voice came from heaven saying,

v.11 *'You are my beloved son'*. These words come from Ps.2.7 — one of the 'royal' psalms associated with the expectation of a kingly Messiah. Jesus knew his communion with God was closer than that of other people.

'with whom I am well pleased'. These words come from Isa. 42.1 and form part of one of the great poems about the suffering servant of the Lord.

So two contrasted ideas are brought together. Jesus seems to have accepted that he *is* the Messiah, but one more like the Suffering Servant that Isaiah had written about than the kind of kingly Messiah the Jews were expecting. Tradition had it that the Messiah would be beyond suffering. A suffering Messiah would have seemed a contradiction in terms. Small wonder that Jesus needed to go away

The Mount of Temptation near Jericho

into the wilderness to work out on his own in meditation what this role might mean in practice.

2. THE TEMPTATIONS

Luke 4.1 – 13: Matt. 4.1 – 11

Be realistic about what happened and try to abandon childhood pictures of a scarlet demon peering round a rock.

Jesus has just had an overwhelming religious experience in which he has been given a new and unexpected understanding of the role of the long-awaited Messiah. Furthermore he has understood that he himself is the Messiah. He now has to work out from a number of options what God requires.

There are three things common to all three temptations:

(i) Each is a temptation to act in a way which, far from appearing wrong, seems in fact to be doing good.
(ii) Each is a temptation to put God to the test — to ask for proof that Jesus had not imagined the staggering experience at his baptism.
(iii) In each case Jesus rebuffs the temptation by quoting scripture — the word of God — and so puts himself under God's authority.

(a) TURNING STONES INTO BREAD

Jesus is weak with hunger. He had been fasting for a long time. Fasting is a way of reinforcing prayer but it is a hard discipline. So the temptation to turn stones into bread is appropriate for three reasons:

(i) The longing to satisfy his real human hunger would make the temptation attractive.
(ii) People expected that the Messiah would produce 'bread from heaven' as Moses had provided manna in the wilderness. Might providing bread in the wilderness be an appropriate Messianic action?
(iii) The opportunity to feed the hungry in Palestine which such a miracle would provide would be in keeping with the concern for people which Jesus constantly showed.

LENT
Christians recall the time Jesus spent in the wilderness during the season of Lent which is a period of six weeks' preparation leading to Easter. The word 'Lent' comes from an Anglo-Saxon word 'lencten' (= spring). The first day of Lent is Ash Wednesday (so called because ashes are a sign of penitence) and the period lasts for forty days, not counting Sundays. Sundays for Christians are a weekly celebration of the resurrection and so are not included in the fasting of Lent. During this time Christians try to improve the level of their own ability to resist temptation and they try to lead God-centred rather than self-centred lives.

TEST YOURSELF ON FACTS

1. Where was Jesus baptised?
2. Christ is a Greek word which means the same as . . . .
3. How do the gospels describe the coming of the Holy Spirit at Jesus' baptism?
4. Jesus heard God speaking to him at his baptism. What did God say?
5. What was Jesus' reply to the devil when he was tempted to turn stones into bread?
6. What had the devil suggested when Jesus answered 'The scripture says, Worship the Lord your God and serve only him'?
7. How did the devil attempt to reassure Jesus that it would be safe for him to jump from the top of the Temple?

Jesus rejects this temptation because:

(a) He never uses his power for selfish reasons
(b) He knows that man has spiritual longings as well as physical needs. These were the aspirations he had come to feed.
(c) He knows that he cannot save people from ultimate physical death. Performing a miracle to feed the hungry would result in incessant calls for him to repeat it and he could spend his whole life turning stones into bread rather than leading people to God.

In verse 4 (in both gospels) Jesus' reply is taken from Deut. 8.3, 'Man shall not live by bread alone.'

(b) PROMISE OF WORLDLY POWER IN EXCHANGE FOR WORSHIPPING THE DEVIL

Remember these temptations are going on in the mind of Jesus. Forget journeys on flying carpets!

This temptation is appropriate for two main reasons:

(i) The Jews were expecting a political Messiah. King David had pushed back his enemies and united the country under his own rule. It was expected that the Messiah would similarly expel the Romans and become the ruler of a free and independent state. Jesus must have given serious thought to the question of whether this was truly God's will.
(ii) The way to seize worldly power is to use evil means — war, violence, deceit. Might the end justify the means?

Jesus rejects this temptation because he realises that God's kingdom cannot come through the devil's means. Love, joy and peace are the hallmarks of God's rule and these cannot be established by force. Instead the minds and hearts of people have to be won through loving them and serving them rather than through compromising with the devil.

In verse 8 (Luke), Jesus' second reply again quotes scripture — 'Worship the Lord your God and serve only him.' (Deut. 6.13). Thus, for the second time, Jesus firmly puts himself under God's authority.

(c) THE PINNACLE OF THE TEMPLE

This experience is again a temptation to put God to the test. ('*If* you are God's son . . .'). In this case the temptation lies in the fact that:

(i) It would seem to be a fulfilment of the prophecy that the Messiah would suddenly come to his temple (Mal. 3.1). Remember that Jesus was a Jew, well versed in Hebrew scripture.

(ii) If he were to throw himself from the Temple and fall unharmed to the brook Kidron about 140 metres below, the sheer wonder of it would inevitably attract a large following to his cause. Was this really what God wanted?

Jesus rejects this temptation because:

(i) Faith in God involves trusting him, not testing him.

(ii) People who are attracted only by wonders will just as quickly run after the next novelty.

In Luke verse 11 notice that the devil himself quotes scripture (Ps.91.11 – 12) for his own ends.

Verse 12 (Luke), Jesus again quotes God's authority — 'You shall not put the Lord your God to the test' (Deut. 6.16) in rejecting this last temptation, but notice in verse 13 that the devil left him only 'for a while.'

Temptations of this kind — to take short cuts, to seek for glory and avoid suffering to give way to selfish wishes — were to return at different times during Jesus' ministry, although never again described so graphically.

Dramatic actions have their place, but were not God's way for the Messiah.

CHECK YOUR UNDERSTANDING

1. *How did Jesus come to realise that he was to be a suffering Messiah?*
2. *Can you suggest why Jesus came to be baptized?*
3. *Can you suggest two things common to all three temptations?*
4. *Why do you think Jesus refused to turn stones into bread?*
5. *Why was it an appropriate temptation to offer Jesus worldly power?*
6. *Why should the devil himself quote scripture?*

WHAT DO YOU THINK?

1. The story of the Temptations is an example of material taken from Q. It does not appear in St Mark's Gospel and there are slight differences between St Matthew and St Luke's use of the material. Examine these differences carefully and suggest reasons for them.
2. Does it matter that the gospels do not agree in all details? Do you think this makes them less reliable as evidence? (If possible watch the News on BBC1 and then on Channel 4. What differences do you notice in the details of the news coverage?)

The Disciples

1. CALL OF THE FIRST FOUR DISCIPLES

Mark 1.14–20: Luke 4.14–15: Matt. 4.18–22

The word 'disciple' means pupil, one who learns. The word 'discipline' comes from the same root. St Mark assumes that his readers will know what had happened to John the Baptist and, the work of the forerunner now being completed, goes straight into the message of Jesus — 'The kingdom of God is near! Turn away from your sins and believe the Good News (v.15 GNB) Notice that it is *Good* News and no longer the austere threats of John the Baptist.

FISHING

The main industry around the Sea of Galilee was fishing. Jesus was to use things which were familiar to his fishermen friends in his teaching. Their nets were to become a symbol of the last judgement, God sorting the good from the bad as the fishermen themselves threw away fish of no value.

They were to become 'fishers of men', this time their nets being a symbol of the church, drawing men from the outside world into the security of its fellowship.

Nowadays, at restaurants around the shore of the Sea of Galilee, pilgrims are served 'Peter's perch', the fish most commonly caught in the lake.

● ***DEATH OF JOHN THE BAPTIST***

Eventually John the Baptist had been silenced. You can read the story in Mark 6.14–29. He had offended Herod Antipas because he had protested at his marrying his brother's wife and consequently had been thrown into prison. The end came almost by accident and through the malice of Herodias, Herod's wife.

The first disciples were fishermen — two pairs of brothers. It seems unlikely that they would leave their nets and follow at the simple call of a passer-by. The Fourth Gospel helps to clarify this point by showing that these men had known Jesus for some time and so had probably been considering throwing in their lot with him before this occasion. This was a moment of personal commitment after a period of acquaintance. The Church sees this not

Fish caught in the Sea of Galilee, seen here being eaten at Tiberias, are known as 'Peter's Perch'.

just as an historical story but as having the following religious implications:

(a) The call to commit themselves to Jesus came in the midst of their everyday work. God's call is not confined to holy people in holy places.

(b) Something had to be sacrificed:
   (i) Simon and Andrew gave up their livelihood
   (ii) James and John sacrificed not only livelihood but also family ties.

(c) Christian discipleship in any generation is likely to start in this way.

2. CALL OF LEVI

Mark 2.13 – 14: Matt. 9.9: Luke 5.27

The next individual to be called was Levi, the tax collector. He would have been a customs officer on the great toll road which ran through Capernaum all the way to the coast.

Again the call comes in the midst of a man's working life and again his response is immediate in leaving all to follow Jesus. The remarkable element in this story is that Jesus called a despised tax collector to join his followers. Not only did Jesus invite Levi to become a disciple but he also sat at table with him and his friends. Going to a meal in someone's home was normally a sign of real friendship, as is still the case. The fact that St Mark and St Luke refer to him as 'Levi' and St Matthew refers to him as 'Matthew' suggests that Levi was given a new name (Matthew means 'Gift of God') following the change in his character which resulted from his association with Jesus — in the same way that Simon was to become 'Peter'.

• *TAX COLLECTORS*

Tax collectors were highly unpopular, not just because nobody likes paying taxes at the best of times, but more importantly because:

1. *They were employed by the Romans who, as the occupying power, were disliked by the Jews.*
2. *They had a reputation of being dishonest. It was difficult to check whether the correct tax had been levied and doubtless many tax collectors did feather their own nests. They were allowed to charge a rate of tax which would provide themselves with a living. Some interpreted this privilege more liberally than others.*
3. *Their work inevitably brought them into contact with Gentiles thus rendering them ritually 'unclean' as far as the Jewish religion was concerned.*

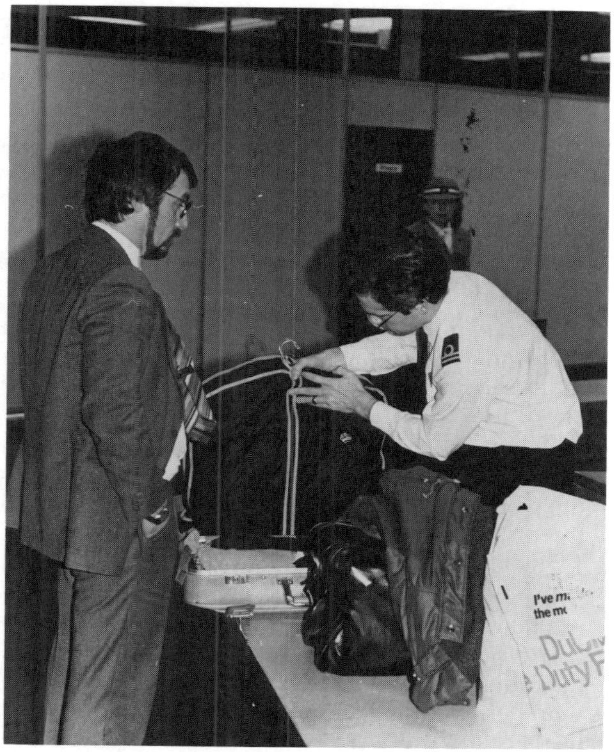

Customs officials are part of the tax system but nowadays see that levies are justly imposed.

3. CALL OF THE TWELVE APOSTLES

Mark 3.13 – 19: Matt 10.1 – 4: Luke 6.12 – 16

St Luke alone tells us that Jesus spent the night in prayer before choosing the twelve apostles. The word 'apostle' means 'one who is sent'.

The number is significant. There had been twelve tribes of Israel, God's specially chosen people. Jesus is about to establish a new people of God and so twelve leaders are chosen to form its nucleus.

The gospels do not agree exactly over their names and we hear very little more about some of them. Taking St Mark's list as our basis, what do we know about these men?

Simon (Jesus gave him the name Peter). St Mark does not make the point that Simon's nickname, Peter, really means 'Rock'. It comes from the Greek word *petra*. In Aramaic (the language spoken by Jesus) it is Kephas. This must have been quite a joke at first. Peter was not a very reliable person but became so through his friendship with Jesus.

James and John — the sons of Zebedee. They too were given a nickname by Jesus. Boanerges means 'men of thunder' and suggests they had stormy temperaments.

Andrew — the brother of Simon. Little is said about him in the Synoptic Gospels but John shows us he was a practical man.

Philip — not much is known about him but you will find stories involving him in John 12.21 and Acts 8.5.

Bartholomew — this is really a surname. Later tradition says that Bartholomew is the same person as Nathaniel, not mentioned in St Mark's list.

Matthew, son of Alphaeus — the tax collector.

Thomas — 'doubting Thomas' who, in the end, was to be the first person after the resurrection to call Jesus 'My Lord and my God'. His name was probably a nickname meaning 'Twin'.

James, the son of Alphaeus — and so presumably brother of Matthew.

Thaddaeus — the least certain of the names. St Luke mentions a different name altogether and some manuscripts call him Lebbaeus. No need to worry about him for GCSE!

Simon the Zealot (or Cananaean). The Zealots were a group of ardent Jewish patriots who wished to overthrow the Roman government — first century freedom fighters.

Judas Iscariot — his name probably means 'Man from Kerioth' but other suggestions have been made e.g. that his name comes from the Aramaic word for 'false', or that it comes from a Latin word meaning 'assassin'. He was, of course, the disciple who betrayed Jesus.

Jesus called these twelve men for two purposes:

(a) 'that they might be with him.'

(b) 'that he might send them forth to preach.'

Before they could go out to preach, they had to '*be with him,*' i.e. know him personally so that they could speak from knowledge and not just from hearsay. They were to be both disciples and apostles and were to be ready to carry on the work of Jesus after he himself had left the world.

4. SENDING OUT OF THE TWELVE

Mark 6.7 – 12: Matt. 10.5 – 15: Luke 9.1 – 6

Eventually the time comes for the disciples to be set to work. Notice the following points:

(a) They are sent out in pairs — perhaps not just for safety but also for mutual encouragement.

(b) Jesus gives them his own authority to heal.

(c) They are to travel light i.e. have faith that their needs will be provided (*learn the list of instructions accurately*).

(d) Where they are not welcomed they are to shake the dust from their feet. Jews did this as they crossed the border into their own country so that the Holy Land would not be contaminated by Gentile dust from their feet.

N.B. St Luke alone tells us of another occasion when Jesus sent out **seventy** (some versions say seventy-two) — see Luke 10.1 – 12. The instructions are similar, though more detailed. Since seventy is a significant Gentile number (there were supposed to be seventy Gentile nations), this mission can be regarded as a mission to the Gentile world.

CHECK YOUR UNDERSTANDING

1. *What is the difference between a disciple and an apostle?*
2. *Why did Jesus call twelve men?*
3. *Can you suggest a possible reason why the four fishermen dropped everything at once to follow Jesus?*
4. *Do you think it important that they had to sacrifice something at the outset? Give reasons for your answer.*
5. *What was remarkable in Jesus calling Levi to be a disciple?*
6. *Why were tax collectors unpopular?*
7. *For what two purposes were the apostles called?*

TEST YOURSELF ON FACTS

1. Where were Simon and Andrew when Jesus called to them 'follow me'?
2. What did Levi do to earn his living?
3. What is the connection between Levi and Matthew?
4. What did Jesus do the night before he called the twelve apostles?
5. Which two apostles had the surname Zebedee?
6. Which two apostles were sons of Alphaeus?
7. What nickname did Jesus give to Simon?
8. Which apostle was Simon's brother?
9. Which apostle betrayed Jesus?
10. Which of the following were among the twelve apostles?
    Peter, John, Mark, Matthew, Luke, Andrew, James, Judas.
11. What did Jesus do to help his disciples when he sent them out?
12. Name three things the disciples were *not* to take with them.

WHAT DO YOU THINK?

1. What kind of person would you be prepared to drop everything to follow?
2. What problems would the disciples have, coming from different backgrounds, in getting on together?

The Authority of Jesus

1. THE AUTHORITY OF JESUS Mark 1.21 – 22

The first story we have of Jesus in action takes place in the synagogue in Capernaum and Jesus is teaching. Since the evangelists obviously recognised the importance of teaching in his ministry, it is perhaps surprising that St Mark tells us so little of what he actually taught. But he stresses the *manner* in which he taught. It was marked by authority, which was instantly recognised by everyone who came into contact with him. Verse 22 describes the amazement of those who heard Jesus speak. The reason why his teaching was not like that of others was that the rabbis taught by quoting and comparing the opinions of other teachers whereas Jesus spoke with an inward, personal authority which was not derived from other people. And the difference was instantly noticed and caused comment. St Mark leaves his readers to draw their own conclusion as to the source of this authority. Having just told the story of the baptism, it should not be difficult for his readers to conclude that the reason lies in Jesus' relationship with God.

BELIEFS CONCERNING THE DEVIL AND SICKNESS

As we begin to look at some of the healing miracles of Jesus we need to understand something of the attitude to illness of his contemporaries. The scientific, medical, geographical knowledge of the gospels belongs to the first century. Sickness was regarded as the work of the devil and mental disorders were believed to be caused by demon possession. As people nowadays do not believe in demons, it is difficult for modern readers to interpret the healings in ways which are meaningful. Yet modern psychiatrists differentiate between mental illnesses caused by a disease of the brain, and disturbances of the total personality when the patient seems to be 'possessed' by some power from the unconscious mind. It remains true that the miracles of healing are the least difficult for us to accept since many people in our own day have experience of the miracle of healing. Normally, of course, healing is brought about through medical science but sometimes there is no logical medically-recognised explanation. It is not the doctor himself but the healing powers of the body which brings about the cure. The doctor helps that process through drugs, surgery, even his bedside manner, but the ability to heal is innate in a living body.

St Mark shows that even those without benefit of this knowledge recognised that the teaching of Jesus was on a plane altogether higher than they had ever heard before.
Furthermore this authority was not confined to words but was to be shown in works as well.

2. HEALING OF THE DEMONIAC
Mark 1.23 – 27: Luke 4.31 – 37

This particular story is an example of an exorcism (= calling out of an evil spirit). The modern medical name for the illness would be 'hysteria'. All the same, St Mark wants to show that the powers of evil recognise Jesus as the Messiah and join battle with him.
v.24 Calling out Jesus' name was an attempt to gain power over him. It was a widely-held belief that knowing the identity of an opponent and calling out his name conferred supernatural power over him.
v.25 The word translated 'Be quiet' is literally 'be muzzled' — a word which implies the binding of a wild animal.
v.27 The main point St Mark is making is the effect on the bystanders. 'This man has *authority* to give orders to the evil spirits, and they obey him.' (GNB)
But notice too that Jesus is *healing on the sabbath* — an issue we shall consider further in Unit 10.

3. SIMON'S MOTHER-IN-LAW
Mark 1.29 – 31: Matt 8.14 – 17: Luke 4.38 – 41

This is a more straightforward story of healing, but remember that it is a *second example of healing on the sabbath*.
St Mark was recording Peter's memories of the ministry of Jesus. Naturally he would vividly remember the healing of his own mother-in-law.
It has been suggested that his mother-in-law may have been suffering from malaria. Luke uses the correct medical term for a high fever but we all know how we feel after a spell in bed with a high temperature. So, is it not remarkable that the old lady got up and began to serve them straightaway? It is also a very human reaction to want to do something to show thanks to someone who has helped us.
The story is immediately rounded off with an account of all the sick being brought to the healer — a reminder of what the background to Jesus' life must have been like all the time.

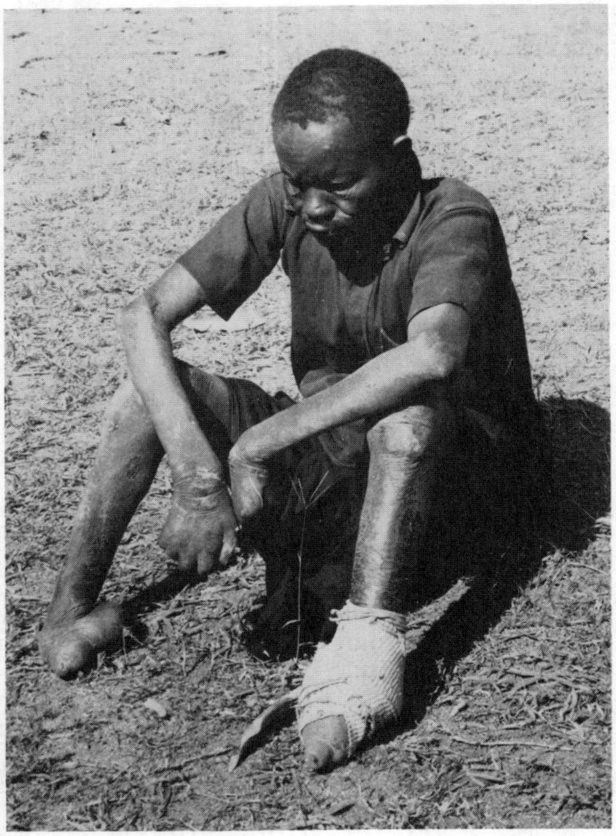

TEST YOURSELF ON FACTS

1. What was Jesus doing in the synagogue when the demoniac approached him?
2. What did the demons cry out?
3. What did Jesus say?
4. What amazed the crowd in this incident?
5. What day of the week was it? (CAREFUL!)
6. What was wrong with Peter's mother-in-law?
7. What did she do after Jesus healed her?
8. What did the leper do when he saw Jesus?
9. What did Jesus do to the leper which was very unusual?
10. Jesus told the leper to do two things. What were they?
11. What did the man do instead?
12. What effect did this have on Jesus?

4. HEALING OF THE LEPER

Mark 1.40 – 45: Matt. 8.1 – 4: Luke 5.12 – 16

The Good News Bible wisely replaces the traditional word 'leper' by 'a man suffering from a dreaded skin disease.' Not all the cases of leprosy recorded in the Bible would have been the disease we know as leprosy. It is worth reading Leviticus chapters 13 and 14 to see the different symptoms of the different kinds of skin diseases and their different treatments — a glimpse of Jewish hygiene regulations. There are many interesting points to notice in this story:

(a) The leper comes running to Jesus. He must have been desperate yet reasonably confident that he would be sympathetically received. The rules required lepers to keep a definite distance away from people and they had to cry out 'unclean, unclean' if anyone accidentally approached them. This was not just because of the risk of passing on a contagious disease. Lepers were regarded as 'unclean' in a spiritual sense too and were forbidden to enter any holy place. It was thought that they passed on their 'uncleanness' to anyone with whom they came into contact. There is a pathetic urgency about his appeal — 'if you want to you can make me clean.'

CHECK YOUR UNDERSTANDING

1. *What was the difference between the teaching of Jesus and that of other teachers?*
2. *What is common to the healing of the demoniac in the synagogue and the healing of Simon's mother-in-law?*
3. *What do you understand by the term 'unclean'?*
4. *What do you understand by the 'messianic secret'?*
5. *What special significance might there be about Jesus healing a leper?*

(b) In verse 41 early versions of the gospels read that Jesus was moved with pity whilst others say he was angry. Obviously he was not angry with the poor leper he was about to help. More probably he was angry at the system which condemned such people to a loveless isolation. Imagine never being able to speak to a soul.

(c) Jesus *touched* him. Imagine the effect on the man of human contact after months or even years of isolation. Normally Jesus would then have been made 'unclean' himself but instead his power cleanses the leper. It is no accident that the command is: 'Be clean' — spiritually and physically. The Bible uses the imagery of being clean to describe spiritual as well as physical wholeness.

(d) In verse 44 Jesus tells the leper to keep quiet about what Jesus has done for him. This unwillingness to have his healings made known is part of what is called the Messianic secret. The healing of lepers was one of the things the Jews expected when the Messiah came but, as we have seen (Unit 7.1 and 2(b)), the Jews were expecting a politically powerful Messiah. Jesus dared not risk an early recognition of himself as Messiah in case they tried to make him king. His ministry would then be in ruins.

(e) Despite not wanting his action to be made known, Jesus obeys the Jewish law in telling the man to go and show himself to the priest. The priests were authorised to declare a leper cured. An offering had to be made because the man was supposed to have sinned and making the offering rid him of guilt. It is important to remember Jesus' obedience to the law in this matter in view of the conflict he was about to experience with the religious authorities.

WHAT DO YOU THINK?

1. Consider what it was about Jesus which helped the healing process in each of the cases considered in this Unit.
2. Healing brings 'wholeness', so mind, body and spirit are all involved. Discuss the influence the three have on each other e.g. if the body is sick, what is the effect on your mind? Find out the meaning of 'psychosomatic illnesses'.

The girl in the wheelchair was helped by friends when the author took a school pilgrimage to Walsingham. She received no medical treatment while there but returned home cured of knee trouble. Would you regard this as a modern miracle?

Conflicts with the Pharisees

Think for a moment what it feels like to be 'picked on'. Some people have the idea that particular teachers are picking on them. Think too of individuals in a class who are picked on by the rest. Why does this happen? Very often the person has done nothing to deserve being treated in this way. In this Unit we are going to examine six stories in which the Pharisees seem to pick on Jesus. Never forget that Jesus was a Jew and so subject to the religious laws of the Jews but Jesus had very definite ideas about which of these laws were truly from God and which had been added over the centuries by men. He was obedient to the former (remember his instruction to the leper he healed (Unit 9.4 (e)), but would not blindly obey the latter. Remember too that Jesus was popular with the ordinary people. His ministry was one of teaching and healing and we are frequently told of the awe and amazement which people felt in his presence. He had done nothing anti-social to deserve being 'picked on'.

A flat roofed house in Palestine.

1. HEALING OF THE PARALYSED MAN AND CLAIM TO FORGIVE SINS

Mark 2.1 – 12: Matt. 9.1 – 8: Luke 5.17 – 26

If you look closely you will find that there is a story within a story here. Read Mark 2.1 – 4 and then go to the second half of verse 10 and read from there to the end. That is a typical healing story. A paralysed man is brought to Jesus by four friends. Jesus tells him to get up, roll up his bed and go home. The man does so and the crowd is amazed and praises God., *Make sure that you can retell the story, paying particular attention to the words of Jesus and the reaction of the crowd.*

It is the section from v.5 – 10a which needs comment.

(a) 'seeing how much faith they had' — whenever Jesus performs a miracle, faith is necessary. It need not be faith on the part of the person to be healed, though often it is — as in the case of the healing of the leper (Mark 1.40). Here the four friends had faith in Jesus sufficient to lead them to make a hole in the roof. The man may have had faith too.

(b) 'Jesus said to the paralysed man, ''My son, your sins are forgiven''' (GNB) — and so seems to imply that the man's paralysis is a punishment for sin. This is totally contrary to what he clearly says on another occasion (Look up John 9.3). Sickness is not a punishment for individual wrongdoing (though, of course, we may have to suffer the consequences of smoking, drug-taking, accidents which happen because of drunken driving etc.). On the other hand, a sense of guilt can produce physical symptoms. We do not know what burden of guilt might have led the paralysed man to give up and take to his bed but Jesus realised he needed to be released from it.

> **HOUSES**
> **Wealthy people probably lived in houses made of stone but the houses of the poor may have been little more than plastered mud, baked hard in the sunshine. The houses consisted of one large room, one end of which was on a higher level. This was used by the family as sleeping quarters, bedding being rolled up and stored along the walls by day. The lower level could be used to house the animals at night or as a workshop by day. Houses had flat roofs, the strong rafters being covered with branches which were then plastered with mud. A roller was kept on the roof and it was the woman's job to go up onto the roof and roll it flat after rain. The steps leading to the roof went up the outside wall. So the damage done by the four friends of the paralysed man would be easily repaired, but notice that St Luke describes the house as being tiled, which would have been the kind of house owned by a wealthier man than Peter. (It is assumed, since this story is set in Capernaum, that Jesus was staying in Peter's house).**

A flat roofed house in Palestine.

within a story here. Read Mark 2.1 – 4 and then go to the second half of verse 10 and read from there to the end. That is a typical healing story. A paralysed man is brought to Jesus by four friends. Jesus tells him to get up, roll up his bed and go home. The man does so and the crowd is amazed and praises God., *Make sure that you can retell the story, paying particular attention to the words of Jesus and the reaction of the crowd.*

It is the section from v.5 – 10a which needs comment.

(a) 'seeing how much faith they had' — whenever Jesus performs a miracle, faith is necessary. It need not be faith on the part of the person to be healed, though often it is — as in the case of the healing of the leper (Mark 1.40). Here the four friends had faith in Jesus sufficient to lead them to make a hole in the roof. The man may have had faith too.

(b) 'Jesus said to the paralysed man, "My son, your sins are forgiven"' (GNB) — and so seems to imply that the man's paralysis is a punishment for sin. This is totally contrary to what he clearly says on another occasion (Look up John 9.3). Sickness is not a punishment for individual wrongdoing (though, of course, we may have to suffer the consequences of smoking, drug-taking, accidents which happen because of drunken driving etc.). On the other hand, a sense of guilt can produce physical symptoms. We do not know what burden of guilt might have led the paralysed man to give up and take to his bed but Jesus realised he needed to be released from it.

Be very careful that you understand the meaning of the word 'sin' in the very precise sense in which the Bible uses it. Sin is an action performed in deliberate defiance of the known will of God. Not every wrong act is necessarily a sin.

(c) 'This is blasphemy. God is the only one who can forgive sins.' Jesus would have agreed that forgiveness comes from God. Remember, however, that the gospels are sacred books of the Church and to Christians Jesus *is* God. This and other healing stories are told to show that God's power is breaking through into the world in the life and work of Jesus.

(d) Notice that the teachers of the law (or 'scribes') are not yet prepared to come out into the open in criticising Jesus. Here '*they thought to themselves*' (GNB). The 'murmuring' is beginning.

> • ***SCRIBES (TEACHERS OF THE LAW/LAWYERS/RABBIS)***
>
> *These were men who devoted their lives to working out what the teachings of the Jewish scriptures really meant. They were not priests and had to earn their living as well as carrying out the duties of a scribe. Their accumulated wisdom was known as the 'Tradition of the Elders' and was passed on by word of mouth from one rabbi to another. By applying the teaching of the law to every detail of everyday life, some apparently ridiculous rules resulted e.g. since work was not allowed on the sabbath, it was a matter of controversy whether it might be breaking the law to eat an egg which a hen had laid on the sabbath. It was this 'Tradition' which Jesus was prepared to ignore when it produced results which were clearly not only unnecessary but even in some instances a burden.*

2. BAD COMPANY

Mark 2.15 – 17: Matt. 9.10 – 13: Luke 5.29 – 32

You will remember that, after Jesus had called Levi, he then went to a meal in his house which was attended by 'a large number of tax collectors and other outcasts.' (Mark 2.15)

This time the opposition becomes bolder. They still do not question Jesus himself but in verse 16 we read, 'they asked *his disciples* "Why does he eat with such people?"'

Their criticism is not based on the kind of social prejudice which might cause raised eyebrows nowadays but on a sense of religious superiority. The Pharisees (whose name means 'separated ones') would have nothing to do with people whose way of life did not come up to their own idea of righteousness. The implication is that Jesus cannot really be a holy person or he would not mix with such people. They assume that Jesus would see things in their way.

> • ***PHARISEES***
>
> *The name seems to date from about 120 BC and means 'separated ones' i.e. those who separated themselves from people who were not religious in the ways of the Pharisees. Although Jesus often criticises them for hypocrisy there were many good and devout men among the pharisees. They were in many ways a party of progress as they wished to make clear for their own times what the laws of Moses required if a man were to lead a good life. However, their devotion to the 'Tradition' of the scribes often led to a rule-keeping approach to religion. They felt as long as they were keeping the rules (many of which they had devised themselves) God would be pleased with them (and they would be able to feel pleased with themselves!) and this led to a preoccupation with external observances. They believed in resurrection and also in angels and were awaiting the coming of the Messiah.*

Jesus replies to their criticism by quoting a proverb 'People who are well do not need a doctor, but only those who are sick.' In other words, 'It is my job to mix with sinners to help them, as a doctor's job is to go to the sick.' St Luke would have had a particular understanding of this saying. A doctor can only help those who *know* they are ill and go to him for help. In the same way Jesus now adds 'I have not come to call respectable people, but outcasts' (GNB) i.e. he cannot help people like the Pharisees who do not recognise that they need his help.

3. FASTING

Mark 2.18 – 22: Matt. 9.14 – 17: Luke 5.33 – 39

This time the criticism is addressed to *Jesus himself* but it is criticism of his disciples, not yet directly of himself. Pious Jews fasted regularly and it was not surprising that Jesus' enemies noticed that his disciples did not. Fasting was a sign of sorrow for sin but Jesus replies that his disciples do not feel like that. They are as happy as people at a wedding. The gospel (= *good* news) should bring joy not gloom.

Jesus then adds two mini-parables:

(a) THE PATCHED COAT

Any housewife knows that if she sews a patch of new, unshrunk cloth onto an old garment, the first time she washes it the patch will shrink and the stitches will tear an even larger hold in the old garment.

(b) WINESKINS

These were made from goatskins. They were treated with tannin and the seams were sealed with pitch. Fresh skins were supple and could take fermenting wine, but they stiffened with age and then the fermentation would cause the wine to burst the skins.

Jesus is saying that the Good News cannot be contained within the rigid framework of the Jewish religion.

4. DISCIPLES AND THE SABBATH

Mark 2.23 – 27: Matt. 12.1 – 8: Luke 6.1 – 5

Now the Pharisees tackle *Jesus himself* about a breach of the sabbath law. The fourth of the ten commandments forbade work on the sabbath. Travellers were allowed to pluck grains of corn as they walked along the fields, but doing so on the sabbath counted as reaping. The sabbath had been intended to give everyone a rest and a time of renewal, servants included. The Pharisees, through their rules, were making it a burden instead of a blessing.

In his reply Jesus points out that King David, the greatest and most admired of the Jewish kings, had allowed his men to eat holy bread when they were hungry and he had put human need above religious practices. (The story is in 1 Sam. 21.1 – 6)

The incident ends with a memorable pronouncement from Jesus. '**The Sabbath was made for man, not man for the sabbath**' and emphasises again the *authority* of the 'Son of Man' in being Lord even of the sabbath.

TEST YOURSELF ON FACTS

1. What was the first thing Jesus said to the paralysed man?
2. What did he say to the teachers of the Law?
3. What did Jesus reply to those who criticised him for eating with tax collectors?
4. What did Jesus say to those who criticised his disciples for not fasting?
5. What story did Jesus tell to those who criticised his disciples for plucking grain on the sabbath?
6. What 'pronouncement' does he make at the end of this episode?
7. What does Jesus say to his critics before he heals the man with the withered hand?
8. What did the Pharisees do afterwards?
9. Who were the scribes?
10. Who were the Pharisees?

5. MAN WITH THE WITHERED HAND (RSV) 'PARALYSED' (GNB)

Mark 3.1 – 6: Matt. 12.9 – 14: Luke 6.6 – 11

It is clear in this fifth story that the enemies of Jesus have set a trap for him, that he sees it for what it is and accepts the danger in the action he takes.

Nobody doubts that Jesus *can* heal. The question is rather *will* he heal on the sabbath? Healing is work and working on the sabbath is forbidden by the religious law. Had the man's life been at risk there

would have been no problem as the law could be broken in such circumstances. The withered hand could have waited till next day, but Jesus heals it and on the sabbath.
v.2 suggests the plotting of Jesus' opponents. Had they come to the synagogue to worship or to catch him out? Probably both.
v.4 Jesus asks them a question they cannot answer without showing up their motives — a technique Jesus was to use many times. He is saying, surely on the sabbath one should be doing *good* (i.e. healing) rather than *evil* (ignoring human need). St Matthew's account of this incident mentions a man being prepared to rescue his animals if they get into difficulties on the sabbath. Surely therefore human need is not to be ignored. By healing, Jesus is fulfilling God's intention for the sabbath, not breaking it.
Having given them the opportunity to protest *before* he heals, Jesus has undermined their chance to criticise him afterwards. Nevertheless (v.6) the religious party of the Pharisees now joins forces with the political party of the Herodians to destroy Jesus.

- ***HERODIANS***

We are not really very sure who the Herodians were but we know they included wealthy people of influence. They were supporters of Herod Antipas and were a political rather than a religious party. They believed in keeping in favour with the Romans. Their opposition probably arose from fear that Jesus would stir up rebellion against Rome.

6. THE BEELZEBUB CONTROVERSY

Mark 3.20 – 30: Matt. 12.22 – 32: Luke 11.14 – 23 and 12.10

Beelzebub = 'Fly-god' and so, to Jews, another name for Satan. Having failed to discredit Jesus in argument, the scribes now suggest his powers come from the devil. Jesus replies with two more mini-parables:

(a) THE DIVIDED KINGDOM

If the devil is driving out demons there must be civil war in his kingdom.

(b) THE STRONG MAN BOUND

Before robbing a house, its owner must be tied up. The power of Jesus is clearly stronger than that of the demons he is casting out.
Jesus then speaks of one sin which is unforgiveable (v.29). He means that if a person is unable to distinguish God's work from the devil's, but really thinks that right is wrong, he cannot be forgiven since the necessary repentance is only possible when a person is aware of having done wrong. These six stories, of course, are just a selection made by the evangelists from many such incidents. They have been chosen to show that opposition to Jesus arose because of his refusal to fit in with the orthodox Jewish life. Jesus later ascribed this to their 'hardness of heart' — a refusal to recognise the power of God at work which eventually leads them to act to destroy him.

CHECK YOUR UNDERSTANDING

1. *What did the teachers of the law mean by saying it was blasphemy for Jesus to forgive sins?*
2. *Why was Jesus criticised for eating with tax collectors?*
3. *Why were the disciples of Jesus not fasting at the time when the Pharisees and the disciples of John the Baptist were?*
4. *What was the meaning of the two mini-parables of the patched garment and the wineskins?*
5. *Why were the disciples not allowed to pluck grain on the sabbath?*
6. *What reasons can you suggest for both religious and political parties joining forces to get rid of Jesus?*
7. *What do you understand by 'the unforgiveable sin'?*

WHAT DO YOU THINK?

1. Do you think it is still necessary to have a day of rest? Give reasons for your answer. Consider the arguments on both sides of the question whether shops should be allowed to open on Sundays.
2. Can you be a Christian without going to Church?
3. Make a list of illnesses which people bring on themselves. Is it reasonable to regard these as being a punishment for sin? Be very precise about what you mean by 'sin'.

More about the Pharisees. Rejection at Nazareth

1. CRITICISM BY THE PHARISEES

Having seen in the last unit the ways in which opposition to Jesus developed, we now turn to consider some of the reasons for it.
Avoid thinking of Jesus and his disciples as the 'goodies' and the scribes and the Pharisees as the 'baddies'. The scribes and the Pharisees were devout Jews, zealous in their upholding of the teaching of the Law. It was their interpretation of that Law which often brought them into conflict with Jesus.

(a) RITUAL CLEANLINESS
Mark 7.1 – 8: Matt. 15.1 – 9

(Notice that in verses 3 and 4 St Mark explains the Jewish customs for the benefit of his Gentile readers. Luke, writing for Gentiles, omits this discussion entirely. Matthew, writing for Jews, omits Mark's explanation.)

• ***THE LAW***

The basis of all Jewish life was the Torah — the 'Law'. This was contained in the first five books of our Old Testament. In these books God had revealed his will for men. It was the duty of men to read the Torah and to learn from it.
The problem was that times had changed since the days of Moses and the Law had to be interpreted anew. Religious people seldom like change and the priests and Saducees (of whom more will be said in Unit 25) saw no point in making changes. They continued to keep the Law exactly as stated.
The scribes and the Pharisees, on the other hand, interpreted the Law in the light of the times in which they were living. They argued fiercely about it and the student was expected to listen to the discussions and to memorise the different teachings of the various rabbis. These explanations were called Midrashim.
By the third century the Law had developed into 613 rules and regulations — 365 'don'ts' and 248 'do's'.

The Law about handwashing had nothing to do with hygiene. It was a matter of ritual cleanliness. A blessing was said at the beginning of meals and it was necessary to come in purity. The washing was an outward sign of this inward purity.
Similarly, food brought from the market place had to be washed in case it had been touched by a Gentile which would defile it and render a Jew who touched it 'unclean'. Jesus' reply, quoting a passage from Isa. 29.13, suggests that the Pharisees have become so obsessed with outward appearances that they have forgotten what the real intention of the Torah was and are giving more weight to the regulations which they themselves have devised.

(b) THE CASE OF CORBAN Mark 7.9 – 13

The fifth commandment is 'Honour your father and your mother'. The Pharisees interpreted this as meaning supporting them when they were old. Children could avoid this obligation by giving their money to the Temple — pronouncing it 'Corban' (an Aramaic word meaning 'dedicated to God'). Jesus calls this hypocrisy.

Presenting the gifts of the people.

(c) THINGS WHICH MAKE A PERSON UNCLEAN Mark 7.14 – 23: Matt. 15.10 – 20

Jesus sums up his attitude to ritual cleanliness by explaining that *things* outside a person cannot make a person unclean. Evil comes from within a person's heart and it is intentions which matter.

2. IN SIMON THE PHARISEE'S HOUSE

Luke 7.36 – 50

In this story we see in action the contrast between the attitude of the Pharisees and that of Jesus.
St Luke, the most vivid storyteller of the four gospel writers, gives us a wonderful picture of Simon, the Pharisee, conscious of his social superiority and of his reputation for religious respectability. The fact that he had not offered the usual courtesies towards a guest — no washing of Jesus' feet on arrival, no kiss of welcome nor perfume for his head — suggests that he felt himself superior to this popular preacher. It was his good deed of the day to invite him to dinner — even though his doing so shows that Simon himself must have been curious to see what this Jesus was like.
How did the woman get in from the street? She was not gate-crashing as we should imagine nowadays. It was usual to leave the doors open at mealtimes so that beggars could enter in search of scraps from the rich man's table. Possibly the woman had heard Jesus preach or seen him healing. Possibly Jesus had helped her personally. We are not told but we know that she was drawn to him and gave an emotional demonstration of her regard for him. Simon the Pharisee is horrified. The woman has a dreadful reputation and he doesn't want people like that in his house. Yet here is Jesus allowing her to weep all over his feet and to dry them with her hair. (Guests left their sandals at the door. Meals were taken reclining at a low table with feet stretched out behind.) Allowing such a woman to touch his feet would make Jesus ritually unclean. He can't be much of a prophet or he would realise what kind of a woman she is.

And that is the difference between Jesus and the Pharisee. Jesus does realise what kind of a woman she *has been* but, whereas Simon the Pharisee sees only a sinner, Jesus sees a *pardoned* sinner. That is the point of the parable he now tells:

vv.41 – 42 **Parable of the two debtors**
Simon is forced to acknowledge that the person who has been let off the greater debt will have the greater love for the man who has written it off. Jesus then gently chides Simon for his lack of welcome and says that the woman's great love shows that she has been greatly forgiven. Notice the order. The forgiveness is not a *reward* for her having shown love. The love is the *result* of her having been forgiven.
The story ends with another pronouncement about the forgiveness of sins (verses 48 – 49) which causes a shock similar to that recorded in the story of the healing of the paralysed man (Mark 2.7 — see Unit 10.1(b) and (c)).

TEST YOURSELF ON FACTS

1. Where would you find the books of the Jewish Law? Name them.
2. Why did Jews wash their hands before meals?
3. How could Jews avoid the duty of looking after their parents?
4. Why was Simon the Pharisee annoyed with the woman in his house?
5. Retell the parable of the two debtors.
6. What does Jesus say has saved the woman?
7. In the parable of the Pharisee and the tax collector at prayer, why is the Pharisee satisfied with himself?
8. What is the name of the town where Jesus was brought up?
9. What did Jesus say after he had read from scripture in the synagogue?
10. What proverb did Jesus expect the people to quote to him?

3. THE PHARISEE AND THE TAX COLLECTOR AT PRAYER Luke 18.9 – 14

Be very careful to remember that this is a parable — a story told by Jesus. It is so vividly written that many students confuse it with something that actually happened. STUDY THE TEXT. This is really a story about two different approaches to God and it well illustrates the risk attached to the Pharisaic way of keeping rules. Naturally Jesus is exaggerating, as good story-tellers must if their stories are to be remembered. Not all Pharisees were like this one.
v.11 Some versions say 'The Pharisee stood and prayed thus *with himself*' i.e. he was not really praying at all. Notice how self-righteous he is and how all his thoughts are on himself ('I. . . I . . . I . . .'). He has done nothing wrong and is proud of the fact. And his pride erects a barrier between himself and God. The tax collector, on the other hand, turns to God, sees himself in God's light and knows himself to be a sinner in need of mercy. So it is the tax collector, who acknowledges his sin, who is 'justified' (= declared acquitted).

We have now seen some of the reasons for Jesus' being rejected by the religious authorities:

(a) He seemed to be a threat to some of their most treasured customs e.g. the laws regarding sabbath observance, ritual cleanliness etc.

(b) He mixed with outcasts i.e. people who did not come up to the Pharisaic standard.
(c) He was outspoken in his criticism when he saw religious hypocrisy.
(d) They feared a Messianic uprising which would bring reprisals from the Romans and might lead to the destruction of the Temple itself.

On the whole, he was popular with ordinary people but there was one occasion when they rejected him. It happened right at the beginning of his ministry and in his own home town of Nazareth.

4. REJECTION AT NAZARETH

Luke 4.16 – 30: Mark 6.1 – 6: Matt. 13.53 – 58

The incident in the synagogue at Nazareth happened early in Jesus' ministry. His fame as a teacher had spread throughout the district and in due course he came to his own home town of Nazareth and went to the synagogue on the sabbath.

The passage which Jesus read was taken from the book of the prophet Isaiah (Isa. 61.1 – 3). Originally the passage referred to the exiles who had been slaves but Jesus in his sermon uses it to mean that he has been sent to do God's work in this way. It was expected that the Messiah would do all the things mentioned (as well as healing lepers — see Unit 9.4(d)).

v.21 is therefore a startling announcement. Jesus is saying the time of the Messiah has come and that the people are seeing the fulfilment of these prophecies in himself. It takes time for the message to sink in.

Notice the stages by which his own people reject him:

(a) 'They were all well impressed with him' (GNB) v.22
(b) Then doubt creeps in — 'Isn't he the son of Joseph?' v.22 i.e. 'Isn't the carpenter's lad getting a bit above himself?'

> ● ***SYNAGOGUES***
>
> *The word 'synagogue' means 'meeting place' and the synagogue is still the centre of a local Jewish Community. A synagogue does not have to be purpose built but must have certain characteristics in it, i.e.:*
>
> *(i) The Holy Ark, facing towards Jerusalem, which contains the Torah (= Holy Scrolls of the Books of the Law).*
> *(ii) The everlasting light.*
> *(iii) The Bimah (= a kind of pulpit) from which services are led, usually sung by the Chazzan (= cantor of the synagogue).*
>
> *Synagogue worship developed among the Jews in exile when they could no longer sacrifice at Jerusalem. The form of worship which grew up was centred on the reading and teaching of the Torah. Other readings from the prophets and psalms were also included.* **There were no sacrifices in the synagogue**. *The readings were given standing but the preacher sat to deliver his sermon. Services were arranged by a group of elders and led by the Chazzan, who was elected by the local community.* **These men were not priests. The work of priests was confined to the Temple in Jerusalem.**

The Central Synagogue, London, as it is today.

v.23 The proverb 'Doctor heal thyself' is more or less the equivalent of our saying 'Charity begins at home' i.e. use your gifts of healing here in your own home town.

CHECK YOUR UNDERSTANDING

1. *What was the Torah?*
2. *What is meant by being ritually unclean?*
3. *What is the meaning of 'Corban'?*
4. *In Mark 7.6 – 9 Jesus quotes from the prophet Isaiah. In what way does he apply the quotation to the Pharisees?*
5. *What indications are there that Simon the Pharisee regarded himself as socially superior to Jesus?*
6. *What is the difference between the way in which Simon the Pharisee sees the woman and the way in which Jesus does?*
7. *In the parable of the Pharisee and the tax collector at prayer, what is meant by saying that it was the tax collector who was 'justified'?*
8. *Suggest three reasons for Jesus being rejected by the religious authorities.*
9. *What do we mean by saying that the passage from Isaiah which Jesus read is Messianic?*
10. *Why did Jesus quote the stories of Elijah and the widow of Zarepath, and Elisha and Naaman in his sermon in Nazareth?*
11. *Why was Jesus unable to perform miracles in Nazareth?*
12. *Why do you think the people of Nazareth failed to value Jesus?*

But the healing miracles require faith and to the people of Nazareth Jesus is just 'the boy next door'. They lack the faith in him which releases God's power.

The real trouble comes in the second half of his sermon which culminates in

(c) 'They were filled with anger' (v.28) and tried to kill him.

Two stories had angered them:
(i) The story of Elijah and the widow of Zarephath (Look it up in 1 Kings 17)
(ii) The story of Elisha and Naaman (Look it up in 2 Kings 5).

Both stories show God's loving care for Gentiles but the suggestion that Gentiles might be included in God's salvation is too much for the people of Nazareth.
This rejection by his own people at the beginning of his ministry is a foreshadowing of Jesus' rejection by the Jewish nation later on.

WHAT DO YOU THINK?
Put yourself in the position of the religious authorities in the time of Jesus (i.e. take no account of your knowledge of what his life was to lead to). Were they justified in seeking to protect the Jews from his influence? Give reasons.

Nature Miracles

So far we have studied five of the healing miracles and shall be looking at five more in the next Unit. Few people are unduly troubled about these. Faith healing is reasonably common in our own times and so is not too hard to accept. But when did you last hear of a huge crowd being fed on five loaves and two fishes with twelve basket of scraps being collected at the end? Or when did you last hear of a storm dying away at a command? The writer of the Fourth Gospel helps our understanding when he calles miracles 'signs'. Signs are *sign*ificant — they have a meaning beyond the obvious one, but we need to 'tune in' if we are to understand. Let's try to tune in to four of the nature miracles.

1. STILLING THE STORM

Mark 4.35 – 41: Matt 8.23 – 27: Luke 8.22 – 25

The first of these startling 'nature miracles' happens on the Sea of Galilee. The lake is notorious for its sudden squalls. The arrangement of the surrounding hills funnels the wind onto the water and even experienced fishermen fear its effect. The points to notice in this story are:

(a) Jesus is asleep although a terrible storm is raging. Probably he has perfect faith in divine power sustaining him.

(b) The disciples are terrified and wake Jesus in a panic. Their lack of faith is all too human.

(c) Jesus commands the storm to be still — 'muzzled' — using the same word he had used in healing the demoniac in the synagogue (Unit 9.2). It is as though he is binding a hostile power.

(d) The disciples are now filled with a different kind of fear. It is better described as 'awe' in the presence of a power they cannot understand. 'Who is this man? Even the wind and the waves obey him!' (v.41 (Mark) GNB)

This story must have been used many times in preaching to the early Christians who were suffering persecution. It must often have seemed to them that God was asleep. Think of the effect on *them* of the words of Jesus 'Why are you frightened? Have you still no faith?' Christ would not save them *from* the storm but he was with them *in* it.

2. WALKING ON THE WATER

Mark 6.45 – 52: Matt. 14.22 – 33

This story is similar in many ways to the story of the stilling of the storm and yet there is an eerie quality about it lacking in the first story.

This time the disciples are on their own in the

middle of the lake and Jesus has gone up into the hills to pray. We are not told that there was a storm but the wind was against them and it was heavy work rowing the boat.

Now think of those Christians enduring the persecution in Rome. Bearing in mind what we said in the previous section, can you see the meaning of this story for them? After all, they were the people for whom Mark was writing his Gospel. Modern Christians also read the story in the light of their own experience. Consider the following points:

(a) The disciples were all aware of being alone and knowing themselves to be hard pressed.
(b) They were all aware of the presence of Jesus coming to them — so much so that they thought they were seeing a ghost.
(c) When Jesus got into the boat with them the wind and their fears subsided.

Apply that experience to the 'storms of life'. It has been the experience of Christians in every generation that they have been granted an awareness of Christ's presence upholding them when the going is tough and in this way they have been enabled to endure terrible hardships.

There is a striking addition in St Matthew's account of the incident which shows this experience in action. Peter — the impetuous, ebullient disciple who could always be relied on to speak or act first and think afterwards — is so carried away by what he has seen that he asks Jesus to call him out of the boat to walk on the water too. 'Come!' answered Jesus and Peter went. Then the inevitable happened. He suddenly realised where he was and what he was doing. Faith gave way to 'common-sense'. In his own power he was helpless and began to sink, but Jesus saved him by taking him by the hand.

Notice what Jesus says in v.31 — 'How little faith you have! Why did you doubt?' (GNB)

The whole story is in fact about faith in Christ.

3. FEEDING OF THE FIVE THOUSAND

Mark 6.30 – 44: Matt. 14.13 – 21: Luke 9.10 – 17

This is the only miracle which is recorded in all four gospels — surely an indication that it was considered to be of the utmost significance.

Read the story carefully and *make sure you can reproduce accurately the conversation between Jesus and the disciples.*

This is really an acted parable. A parable is a story which has a spiritual meaning beyond the immediate and obvious one. To help you understand the significance of this story, consider the following six points:

(a) When Moses led the Israelites out of slavery in Egypt through the wilderness, God fed his people on manna (Look up the story in Exod. 16). It was expected that the Messiah would also produce manna in the wilderness i.e. would nourish his people as he led them.

In early art forms (like this fifth century mosaic in a church near Capernanum) the Eucharist is represented not, as you might expect, by bread and a chalice of wine, but by loaves and fishes. So the connection between the feeding miracles and the Eucharist was understood in the very earliest days of the Church.

(b) Remember that sharing a meal with someone is a sign of close friendship. Jesus is treating these 5000 people as close friends and is feeding them in the wilderness as God had done in the time of Moses.
(c) Look at the actions of Jesus. He took the bread . . . gave thanks . . . broke . . . and gave to the people. These are the actions he was to perform at the last supper (Unit 26) and they are the actions which are performed at the central act of Christian worship (called variously Holy Communion / the Eucharist / the Mass / the Lord's Supper). In this act of worship Christians believe that God is coming to them in a very special way and is feeding them with himself. There is therefore a strong link between this story and the feeding which takes place at Holy Communion.
(d) Notice the orderly way in which the crowd sits down in rows, in groups of fifty or a hundred. It is more like a Church service than a picnic and again this points to the connection between this story and Holy Communion.
(e) There were *five* loaves and *twelve* baskets of scraps — both significant numbers for the Jews. (*Five* books of the Law and *twelve* tribes of Israel). This must be a significant Jewish occasion.
(f) In the Old Testament the age of the Messiah is likened to a banquet to which his people will be invited. Jesus is now fulfilling their expectation.

TEST YOURSELF ON FACTS

1. What did Jesus say to his disciples after he had stilled the storm?
2. What did the disciples then say to each other?
3. What did the disciples think when they saw Jesus walking on the water?
4. What happened when he got into the boat with them?
5. In the story of the feeding of the 5000, how many loaves were there? How many fishes?
6. In the story of the feeding of the 4000, how many loaves were there? How many fishes?
7. What were the crowd told to do in both stories?
8. What actions did Jesus perform in both stories?
9. How many baskets of scraps were left over in the story of the feeding of the 4000?

CHECK YOUR UNDERSTANDING

1. *What do we mean by a 'nature miracle'?*
2. *In the story of the stilling of the storm the disciples show two different kinds of fear. What were they?*
3. *What lesson would the story of Jesus walking on the water have had for Christians in Rome in the first century?*
4. *Which story in the Old Testament helps us to understand the meaning of the two feeding miracles?*
5. *Name two other occasions when the actions — take, give thanks, break, give — are significant.*
6. *Why might we assume that the feeding of the 5000 had a Jewish significance?*
7. *Why might we assume that the feeding of the 4000 had a Gentile significance?*
8. *Look up the account of this miracle in the Fourth Gospel (John 6.1 – 13). What extra details are we told?*
9. *Make a list of the similarities between the two feeding miracles.*

4. FEEDING OF THE FOUR THOUSAND

Mark 8.1 – 10: Matt. 15.32 – 39

St Mark (followed by St Matthew) includes a very similar story in which Jesus feeds 4000 people. Some scholars think it is a duplicate story of the previous feeding miracle. If however you are prepared to consider the symbolic meaning of the miracles, certain differences between them suggest a different meaning and a different occasion.

(a) This time there are *seven* loaves and a few fish and *seven* baskets of scraps are collected at the end. Whereas *five* and *twelve* were very significant numbers for Jews, *seven* is significant for Gentiles (e.g. there were seven deacons in the early church, the Gentile world was supposed to be divided into seventy nations).

(b) The word used for 'basket' in the feeding of the 5000 is *'kophinos'* = a basket used by poor Jewish people in Rome whereas the word translated 'basket' in the feeding of the 4000 is *'spyris'* = an ordinary fish basket. It is unlikely that the use of the two different words is accidental.

We are probably not far wrong then in concluding that, in the same way that the feeding of the 5000 is an acted parable of the coming of the Messiah to the Jewish people, this story of the feeding of the 4000 expressed the belief that the Messiah has come for Gentiles as well as Jews.

WHAT DO YOU THINK?

1. Do you find these stories hard to believe? Look again carefully at the actions and reactions of the disciples in each of the four stories. Do they reflect your own feelings? What did the early Christians find in the stories? Why did they tell them? They did not try to explain away the miracles in the life of Jesus but looked for the significance of them. What do you find significant in the stories studied in this Unit?
2. Is it necessary to believe that the stories are accounts of historical events for them to have significance?

Relations with Gentiles

Now let's turn to the healing miracles involving Gentiles. To experience the impact of these stories you are going to need to exercise some historical imagination. Try to put yourself in the place of a first century Jew, a member of a small race who, for religious reasons, was not allowed contact with Gentiles. Such contact would leave a Jew 'defiled'. Furthermore, even though the Jews were a conquered race living under Roman rule, they felt themselves to be superior to other races because of their knowledge of God. Other races, of course, did not share the Jews' view of their own superiority and, at times, insults would fly. National identity was important and no Jew would willingly step out of line to have contact with Gentiles. Remember Jesus was a Jew. This is the background against which these stories must be read.

1. HEALING OF THE SYRO-PHOENICIAN WOMAN'S DAUGHTER

Mark 7.24 – 30: Matt. 15.21 – 28

Jesus travels North to the region of Tyre and Sidon — Gentile territory. He tries to remain incognito but to no avail. A woman hears of his arrival and comes to plead with him on behalf of her sick daughter. Much of the interest in this story centres on the extraordinary conversation which precedes the miracle.

Pay particular attention to the following points:

(a) Jesus' remark about 'the dogs' in (Mark) verse 27 sounds uncharacteristically rude and unhelpful — so much so that the remark is generally taken as proof that the story is absolutely genuine! It is hardly a conversation one would invent to recommend the hero of one's book. By 'the children' Jesus means the Jews. 'The dogs' are therefore Gentiles. The woman knew that this was the way in which Jews referred to them and was unlikely to become unduly upset by the name, particularly if it were used with gentleness.

(b) But why should Jesus apparently be unwilling to heal a sick child? It seems he must have mapped out his Messianic mission to the Jews but has not yet decided that his mission is to include Gentiles.

(c) The mother's witty reply seems to have brought about a change of heart on the part of Jesus and he praises her **faith** and **persistence**. She accepts that the Jews come first for the Messiah but is not discouraged from continuing to plead for her child.

(d) This is the first occasion in St Mark's Gospel when Jesus **heals at a distance**. The mother's persistence and faith release healing for her daughter and the daughter does not come on the scene at all.

2. HEALING OF THE DEAF MUTE

Mark 7.31 – 37

The Greek word used here means 'one who speaks with difficulty'. Some scholars translate the word as 'dumb' or 'mute'; others think the man may have been a stammerer.

The language Jesus spoke was Aramaic (NOT Arabic — *be careful!*) and we seem to be very close to Peter's lively storytelling to young Mark when he records the actual words Jesus used in the language which came naturally to his own tongue. You need to learn these words Jesus actually spoke (and how to spell them). Points to notice in this story are:

(a) The ten towns (or Decapolis) area mentioned in verse 31 is Gentile territory.

(b) Laying hands on him (v.32) is the gesture which normally accompanies the ministry of healing.

(c) Jesus' use of saliva in verse 33 is in line with the medical practice of his times. Saliva was thought to have curative properties (do you

TEST YOURSELF ON FACTS

1. What did Jesus say to the Gentile woman who asked him to heal her daughter?
2. What did the woman reply?
3. What language is the word 'Ephphatha'?
4. What did Jesus do when he healed the deaf stammerer?
5. What did the Jewish elders say to Jesus to recommend that he should help the centurion's servant?
6. What did the Roman centurion say when Jesus was not far from his house?
7. What did Jesus then say to the crowd?
8. Where did the Gerasene madman roam?
9. What effect did seeing the madman healed have on the people?
10. What did Jesus say to the healed madman?
11. What did Jesus tell the ten lepers to do?
12. What was the race of the one who returned to say thank you?

suck your finger if you cut it? What do animals do if they have a sore?) Possibly Jesus is helping to boost the man's faith by his actions.

(d) Verse 34 Jesus looked up to heaven and groaned i.e. he prayed.

(e) Learn the word 'Ephphatha', its spelling and its meaning (= be opened).

(f) Following the healing Jesus tries to prevent news of it spreading. He does not want to be proclaimed as Messiah (why not?) but the whole incident recalls Isaiah 35.5 – 6 (GNB)
('The blind will be able to see,
and the deaf will hear.
The lame will leap and dance,
and those who cannot speak will
shout for joy'.)

— a prophecy of the coming of the Messiah which Jesus is clearly fulfilling.

3. HEALING OF THE CENTURION'S SERVANT

Luke 7.1 – 10: Matt. 8.5 – 13

Luke, as always, gives us the most vivid portrait of the central character in this story. A centurion was a Roman officer in charge of a hundred men. This particular centurion is remarkable for a number of reasons:

(a) He cared enough about his servant to take steps to have him healed. Since slaves could be bought cheaply in the market it would have been unusual to find a soldier going to so much trouble to save a slave's life.

(b) He was a sensitive man. He realised that an officer in the occupying army might not be sympathetically welcomed by a Jewish rabbi, so he asks Jewish friends to speak to Jesus on his behalf.

(c) We learn from these Jewish friends that he had been generous to the Jews and had given them money for a synagogue. Possibly he himself was interested in the Jewish religion although not prepared to be converted to it.

(d) In verse 7 (Luke) we have another glimpse of his sensitivity towards the Jewish people. He realised that a Jew would be unwilling to go to the house of a Gentile (because of 'defilement') and so asks Jesus to heal the slave at a distance and *obviously has faith in his power to do so.*

(e) His comments about authority are also important. They show that *he recognises Jesus as a man of authority*. He knows that his own authority as a centurion comes from a superior and that with that authority he can command those beneath him. He sees a similar chain of command in Jesus. In other words, he is aware, without necessarily understanding, that the power of God is coming into the world through Jesus (Compare the healing of the demoniac in Mark 1.23 – 27 and the comments in Unit 9.2).

Verse 9 (Luke) gives us a rare glimpse of Jesus' own reaction. He was astonished by the man's faith and amazed to find it in a Gentile who inevitably lacked the background knowledge of scripture which should have helped Jews to recognise him as Messiah.

CHECK YOUR UNDERSTANDING

1. *What qualities of character does the Syro-Phoenician woman show which result in the healing of her daughter?*
2. *What is unusual about the healing?*
3. *Why does Jesus tell people not to proclaim his healing of the deaf stammerer?*
4. *Why did the centurion ask Jewish elders to approach Jesus on his behalf?*
5. *Why does the centurion speak of authority?*
6. *What is unusual about the healing of the centurion's servant?*
7. *How do we know Jesus was in Gentile territory when he healed Legion (Mob)?*
8. *Why did the man say his name was 'Legion' (Mob)?*
9. *Why did the demons possessing 'Legion' cry out Jesus' name?*
10. *In what way does Jesus' command to the madman differ from his usual practice?*

4. HEALING OF LEGION (GNB 'MOB')

Mark 5.1 – 20: Matt. 8.28 – 34: Luke 8.26 – 39

There is a difficulty in this story in which Jesus untypically destroys pigs which were farmers' property but, as usual, there is more in the incident than immediately meets the eye. Look again at the comments made on the healing of the demoniac (see Unit 9.2). Many of them apply to this story too. Then take note of the following additional points:

(a) The story is obviously set in Gentile territory. Pigs are 'unclean' animals to the Jews and would never be kept on Jewish soil.

(b) Verse 9 (Mark) — using someone's name was a way of gaining power over him — something the demons had been trying to acquire in verse 7.

(c) The name 'Mob', given in the Good News Bible translation, although it gives the idea of a large number of wild spirits, misses the possible connection with Roman legions (= 6000 men). They were an 'occupying force' as the demons had taken over the mind of the madman.

(d) What about those pigs? It has been suggested that the paroxysms of the madman frightened the pigs and caused them to stampede thus providing Jesus with a 'visual aid' to reassure the madman that he was cured and that his illness would not return.

(e) More importantly, notice that, when people came to see for themselves what had happened, they were more concerned about the loss of their pigs than about the amazing cure of their fellow human being and they ask Jesus to leave. *Would this still be our reaction?* (Think what they missed by driving him away.)

> • ***SAMARITANS***
>
> *Samaritans were regarded as enemies by the Jews. The trouble had started in the seventh century BC. At that time the northern part of Palestine had been conquered by the Assyrians. The Assyrians used to reduce the danger of rebellion in the lands they conquered by moving part of the population elsewhere and importing other races to the newly-conquered territory. The Samaritans were descendants of Jews who had inter-married with foreigners during that period and they now formed a separate people living in the middle of Palestine. Jews from the north travelling to Jerusalem were in danger of attack when travelling through Samaria and it was not unusual to make a detour to avoid passing through Samaritan villages.*
>
> *Jesus consistently taught that this enmity was wrong. He made a Samaritan the hero of one of his best-known parables. It was a Samaritan among the ten lepers who returned to thank him for his healing.*

(f) The man who has been healed is not allowed to follow Jesus. He, in fact, becomes a missionary to his own people. Pay particular attention to Jesus' words in v19 (Mark), 'Go back home to your family and tell them how much the Lord has done for you and how kind he has been to you.' (GNB)

This incident is significant for two main reasons:

(i) It shows Jesus' contact with Gentiles.

(ii) It demonstrates his healing powers.

5. HEALING OF TEN LEPERS Luke 17.11 – 19

In the last of this group of healing miracles Jesus is once again confronted by leprosy (see Mark 1.40–45 in Unit 9.4).

Read the story. Remember the comments made about the previous healing of a leper and then notice the following unusual features:

(a) When all go off, as instructed, to show themselves to a priest, just one turns back to thank the healer. We are not told why the others did not, so *be careful not to invent reasons in an examination answer*. The point that matters is that they failed to say 'thank you' and so failed to make personal contact with Jesus.

(b) Because one had cared enough to want to make contact with Jesus, Jesus says 'Your faith has saved you.' Salvation meant more than physical healing. It is wholeness of mind, body and spirit and this only came when he turned in gratitude to the healer.

(c) The one who turned back was a Samaritan — a race despised by the Jews.
Does counting our blessings make us more aware of them?

SUMMARY

Analyse all the miracles you have so far studied, then copy this chart and complete it.

MIRACLE	MEANS OF HEALING	FAITH SHOWN BY WHOM	WORDS SPOKEN BY JESUS	JEW OR GENTILE?	SABBATH?	SECRET?
Syro-Phoenician Woman's daughter	At a distance	Mother	Let us first feed the children ... dogs?	Gentile	No	No instruction given

UNIT 14

Parables

One of the most useful gifts a teacher can possess is the art of storytelling. Think for a moment how often you remember an anecdote even if you forget the point it was intended to illustrate. That fact is the key to understanding the purpose of the parables of Jesus. Jesus did not invent the parable form. It was a popular way of teaching among the rabbis and there are parables in the Old Testament (e.g. Judges 9.7 – 15; 2 Sam. 12.1 – 4). But Jesus was a superb story teller and he brought the art of the parable to perfection.

1. WHAT IS A PARABLE?

Be careful not to say 'an earthly story with a heavenly meaning'. You need to be more precise than that.

(a) **A parable is a vivid comparison** — a like-saying — which conveys a truth in story form. Abstract ideas are difficult to grasp. Jesus had many things to teach which involved abstract ideas — faith, persistence, forgiveness, kindness — and clothing these ideas in stories made them easier to understand. So, when Jesus wanted to say that the joy which his disciples were experiencing through their new life with him could not be fitted into the outward forms of the Jewish religion, he said 'You can't put new wine which is still fermenting into old wineskins. They are too stiff and will split.' Everybody knew about wineskins. From that knowledge most would understand what he was driving at.

(b) The shortest parables may be little more than **similes or metaphors** e.g. 'You are like salt for all mankind. But if salt loses its saltiness, there is no way to make it salty again. It has become worthless, so it is thrown out and people trample on it.' (Matt. 5.13 GNB)

(c) The longest parables are **fully developed stories**. *Because they are so vividly told be very careful to remember which stories are parables and which are events which actually happened. It is easy for the unwary to become confused.*
It is important to remember that the true parable has **one main point** and that the details — such as vivid character portrayal — are there as part of the storyteller's art to hold our interest and we should not hunt around for meanings in every aspect of the story.

(d) Sometimes parables have been used so often for teaching that preachers and teachers have eventually turned them into **allegories**. In an allegory the details in the story each have meanings and this can obscure the story and make it rather long and dull.

2. WHY DID JESUS TEACH IN PARABLES?

(a) Our first answer is likely to be 'to make his meaning clearer'. Sometimes this is true. When he wants to tell us about God's loving concern for those who have strayed away from him, Jesus takes a situation with which his listeners would be very familiar — the shepherd who has lost a sheep, for example — and builds up a story to which ordinary people can relate (Luke 15.4-6)

(b) Sometimes, however, he seems to tell parables to hide his real meaning. This seems strange in a teacher but, in the Sermon on the Mount, he says that you do not cast pearls before swine or give holy things to the dogs. He must often have had people in the crowds who would scoff at what he had to say and so spoil it for others. On these occasions, by telling a vivid story, he would entertain the crowd with the surface meaning of the tale and yet, for those 'with ears to hear' i.e. those who were attuned to the deeper level of what he was saying, there was profound teaching. We often find that he explains the meaning of the parables in greater detail to his disciples after the crowds have gone away (e.g. the parable of the sower in Mark 4.13-20). So, teaching in parables enabled Jesus to communicate at several different levels simultaneously.

(c) A third reason why Jesus taught in parables is that many of his hearers were not ready to receive the teaching he was giving. It is human nature to forget information which has no immediate relevance. Learning to cook a meal

CHECK YOUR UNDERSTANDING

1. *What is a parable?*
2. *How does a parable differ from an allegory?*
3. *Give three reasons why Jesus may have taught in parables.*
4. *Look up the ten commandments in Exod. 20. Is the summary of the Law given by the scribe a good one?*
5. *Who were the Levites?*
6. *What was the point of Jesus making a Samaritan the hero of his story?*
7. *Do you think the teacher of the law was pleased with what Jesus had said to him? Give reasons.*
8. *Suggest two possible interpretations of the parable.*

takes on a fresh importance if your mother is about to go into hospital. By telling stories there was always the chance that the story would be remembered and that its meaning would become clear when the individual was ready to absorb its lesson. It follows from this that parables will 'speak' to the same individual in a different way as circumstances change.

3. WHERE DID THE STORIES COME FROM?

(a) Jesus uses the experiences of ordinary everyday life which his listeners would know well — a farmer sowing seeds; the unemployed hanging around all day in the hope of finding work in the vineyard; a neighbour hammering on the door long after bedtime asking to borrow some bread.

(b) He also uses folk tales which would be familiar to his hearers but gives them a new twist — the story of the Rich Man and Lazarus (Luke 16.19–31) is a case in point.

(c) Another source of teaching lay in the foibles of human nature which Jesus observes and uses to make his point — a judge who has to be bribed to give a favourable verdict; a dishonest steward who, seeing he is about to be sacked, cheats his master still more so that his master's creditors will feel under an obligation to him once he is out of work; a rich and entirely self-centred man building himself bigger and bigger barns to store his crops little thinking that he is about to die.

4. THE GOOD SAMARITAN Luke 10.25–37

Before studying the parable in detail, notice that it is Jesus' reply to a catch question. One of the scribes (teachers of the law) asks him a question to which he thinks he already knows the answer. 'Teacher, what must I do to receive eternal life?' To a Jew eternal life was a prize to be won by keeping the Law of Moses. It would be a revealing exercise to see how far this Jesus of Nazareth could explain the Law.

As so often, Jesus replies by first asking a question and the scribe then has to show that he already knows the answer to his own question.

Verse 27 combines two Old Testament commandments — love God (Deut. 6.5) and love your neighbour as yourself (Lev. 19.18), a well-known summary of the Law.

The questioner then tries to justify himself by asking 'Who is my neighbour?' To a Jew one's neighbour was not the man next door but one's fellow Jew. Gentiles certainly would not be included among those whom one should help; Samaritans even less so. Instead of entering into a dry academic debate about one's obligations to other people, Jesus tells one of his best known parables.

The road from Jerusalem to Jericho is about 30 kilometres long and it drops about 1000 metres in that distance. Halfway down stands an inn which is now known as the inn of the Good Samaritan. At first the road descends in big sweeps and curves

Desert track in Judean Desert near Jericho.

but shortly before the inn it runs uphill a little way and goes over a ridge. Turning at the top of this ridge a traveller can see a long way back along the way he has come and could spot people coming in the distance. That short uphill run was a favourite spot for muggers. It is easier to attack someone going uphill and there is a sharp drop where bodies could be toppled over and lost. That is the scene of the attack described in verse 30.

First along the road comes a priest, the representative of religion. He sees the wounded man and passes by on the other side. Several excuses can be made for him:

(a) If he were to touch the crumpled heap of humanity and find the man dead, he would become ritually unclean and would have to spend time in purifying himself when he reached Jericho.

(b) There was a very real danger that the mugger was lying in ambush for the next traveller, the priest himself.

Second on the scene is the Levite. He too passes by on the other side and the same 'excuses' can be made for him.

- ***PRIESTS***

Men born into the tribe of Levi qualified as priests. It was not a matter of a boy choosing his own career. Priests were responsible for the worship in the Temple at Jerusalem and were the only people allowed to make animal sacrifices.

- ***LEVITES***

These were assistants to the priests who were responsible for the 'housekeeping' of the Temple. They also formed the choir in the Temple.

Last on the scene comes the Samaritan. Look again at what was said about Samaritans in Unit 13.5. Imagine the impact on the self-satisfied scribe of hearing that a despised Samaritan is the hero of the story. Notice too how Luke, the physician, tells us the treatment given to the wounded man — oil to cleanse and wine to disinfect his wounds (v.34). Even after taking him to the inn, the Samaritan does not leave the man friendless but promises to return and settle any further debt incurred by the innkeeper in caring for him. He goes far beyond what could be expected of a normally sympathetic stranger.

Think carefully about how this parable strikes you personally. It can be interpreted in a number of ways. There is no single 'correct' meaning. Here are some suggestions:

(a) It teaches the obligation to be kind to one another.

(b) It is anti-racist.

(c) It is a comment on putting the outward forms of religion before ordinary human need — being 'so heavenly-minded that one is of no earthly use.'

(d) There is also a popular allegorical interpretation which sees the Good Samaritan as Jesus coming to help the human race, but this interpretation is probably the work of the later Church. Remember that a parable has *one main point*. Searching to find it is the object of teaching in parables. Doing so makes us think.

TEST YOURSELF ON FACTS

1. What question did the teacher of the Law ask Jesus?
2. How did the man summarise the Law?
3. What did the teacher of the law say to justify himself?
4. Where was the traveller in the parable of the good Samaritan travelling from and to?
5. What had the robbers done to him? — say in detail.
6. Who was the first person to come along?
7. Who was the second person to come along?
8. What did they both do?
9. Who came along next?
10. How did he feel when he saw the wounded man?
11. What did he do to help him?
12. What did he say to the innkeeper?
13. What question did Jesus ask the teacher of the law at the end of the story?
14. What did he reply?
15. What did Jesus then tell him to do?

WHAT DO YOU THINK?

Take any fairy tale with which you are familiar e.g. *Cinderella*. What deeper meaning can you find in it?

Three Parables of Forgiveness: Luke 15

The next three stories tell us of God's loving care for those who have turned away from him. All three follow a common pattern which you need to remember.

LOSS — SEARCH — CELEBRATION

```
              2.
       1. L O S S
              E
              A
3. C E L E B  R A T I O N
              C
              H
```

Notice to whom Jesus is speaking. The Pharisees had been criticising him for making friends with people they despised. Remind yourselves what Jesus had said to them on the same subject on another occasion (Mark 2.17 — Unit 10.2)

1. THE LOST SHEEP

Try not to picture the shepherd as someone in a stained glass window. Shepherds have to be tough. They have to be out in all weathers and, in biblical Palestine, had to be prepared to defend their flocks against wild animals. Shepherds in Palestine do not use sheep dogs. They walk ahead of their sheep, call them and the sheep recognise the voice of their own shepherd and follow him.

> ***CHECK YOUR UNDERSTANDING***
> 1. *Can you work out what it is that Jesus was really saying to the Pharisees who criticised him for being a friend of sinners?*
> 2. *What does it tell us of (a) the shepherd (b) the woman (c) the father, that they went to so much trouble to find what was lost?*
> 3. *What lessons did the prodigal son learn from his experience (a) abroad (b) on his return?*
> 4. *In what way is the older brother 'lost' too? In what ways is he like the ninety-nine sheep in the first parable? In what ways is he different?*

This is still the case in that part of the world. There are four points to notice:

(a) The shepherd goes out to search for the lost sheep.
(b) When he finds it, he doesn't drive it home but picks it up and carries it — helps it along.
(c) The ninety-nine sheep are not neglected. They are feeding in the pasture.
(d) The shepherd summons his friends to celebrate.

2. THE LOST COIN (NEB 'SILVER PIECE')

This time it is a coin that is lost. Don't think of the housekeeping money in a purse. It is more likely that Jesus had in mind the woman's dowry. This was made up into a piece of jewellery which she wore around her head.

The message of this story lies in the celebration. God is willing to forgive and rejoice at the lost being restored in a way that the Pharisees, to whom Jesus is speaking, are not.

3. THE PRODIGAL SON (NEB 'LOST SON')

This is really a parable of the father's equal treatment of the two sons. Both sons were lost to him. The younger son had gone off selfishly to enjoy himself *and the father had left him free to go.* (Look also at the story in Unit 20.1 where Jesus offers a rich young man the opportunity of following him but leaves him genuinely free to walk away). The younger son left of his own free will. When bad times came, he had to take a job feeding pigs. For a Jew this would be ignominious as pigs are regarded as 'unclean'. The fact that pigs were being bred at all suggests that the young man had gone away into Gentile territory, thus emphasising his total separation from his family. He seems to have decided to return home as much for selfish reasons as out of regard for his father but, as soon as the father sees him returning, he goes out to meet him to make it easy for him to return.

Verse 22 — the best robe was a sign of honour; the ring a sign of authority; shoes a sign of a free man — slaves went barefoot.

Happy reunion of Dr David Jacobson (following his release from being a hostage), with his son Paul. 'Your brother was dead, but now he is alive; he was lost, but now he has been found.' — GNB.

The son is restored to full sonship and is not treated as a servant which is the best he had hoped for. The older brother is jealous and self-righteous and in a way just as 'lost' to his father as the younger boy. The father goes out to meet him too to try to help him back to a loving relationship. The older brother scornfully refers to 'this son of yours' and is gently rebuked by the father, 'your brother here.' He is given the reassurance 'You are always with me, and everything I have is yours.'

Look back to Unit 6 and notice how, in Christian baptism, Christians believe they become 'inheritors of the kingdom'. N.B. **We are not told whether the older brother went in to join in the celebration.**

TEST YOURSELF ON FACTS

Hunt through the square to find answers to the following questions. Read from left to right, from top to bottom or diagonally.

C	X	U	S	E	A	R	C	H	P	R
O	E	Q	H	F	O	U	N	D	R	O
I	Q	L	O	S	T	R	A	L	O	B
N	S	W	E	E	P	S	L	M	D	E
P	H	B	S	B	O	N	I	F	I	F
A	E	P	T	U	R	W	V	O	G	A
S	E	T	A	B	I	A	E	R	A	T
T	P	J	O	Y	N	C	T	G	L	H
U	Z	R	P	I	G	S	B	I	S	E
R	G	E	N	T	I	L	E	V	O	R
E	S	R	E	P	E	N	T	E	N	N

1. A man had a hundred . . . . . .
2. He . . . . . . one of them
3. He went to . . . . . . for it
4. Where did he leave the ninety-nine?
5. What was lost in the second parable?
6. What does the woman do until she finds it?
7. There is . . . . . . among the angels of God over one sinner who repents.
8. Who is the subject of the third parable?
9. When he fell upon hard times he found a job feeding . . . . . .
10. This suggests he was living in . . . . . . country.
11. Who went out to meet him?
12. The father wanted to . . . . . . him.
13. The son needed to . . . . . .
14. What three things did his father order to be brought?
15. The father told the elder brother 'this brother of yours was dead but is . . . . . . again; he was lost and now he is . . . .
16. All three parables end with a . . . . . .

WHAT DO YOU THINK?

1. Was the father right to allow his son to go away in the first place?
2. Write a modern version of the parable of the Prodigal Son. Think carefully about the characters involved before you start. Which character do you think you yourself would be most like in this situation? Go on — be honest! Can you see how teaching can still be given through parables?

Parables of the Kingdom

We are going to study the parables of the kingdom in the form in which they appear in chapter 13 of St Matthew's Gospel. If your syllabus is confined to a different Gospel, you will find that the comments in this Unit will still apply. In addition we shall look at the parable of the seed growing secretly which only appears in St Mark's Gospel.

1. THE KINGDOM OF HEAVEN (GOD)

The titles 'kingdom of heaven' and 'kingdom of God' are interchangeable. For Jews the name of God was so holy that they avoided using it at all and got round the problem by referring to 'heaven' when they really meant 'God'.

What did they mean by the kingdom of heaven? It is a difficult question but for GCSE we need only consider a few basic points.

(a) The kingdom of heaven is not a geographical place. It is not a place above the sky with pearly gates, a sapphire throne and crystal seas. All this imagery comes from the richness of the Jewish imagination and it can be hard for prosaic Western twentieth century Gentiles to absorb it.

(b) The idea of the kingdom of God is easier to grasp if we think of the king*ship* of God. The kingdom of God then becomes everywhere where God is king. That will include this world as well as the next. So the kingdom of heaven is partly present here and now.

(c) On the other hand, the kingdom of heaven is *also* in the future. It was believed that God would act, and soon, to show his authority and to bring everything under his rule. The gospel writers believed that the kingdom of heaven in this sense was beginning to come in the life and teaching of Jesus. His disciples did not expect this world to last much longer.

(d) If all this seems too difficult, remember it was also too difficult for the people who first heard about it from the lips of Jesus himself. That is why he spoke in parables. For most of us the teaching becomes clearer if we concentrate on what it means to be citizens of the kingdom of heaven, under the king*ship* of God, without becoming bogged down in defining the kingdom itself.

TEST YOURSELF ON FACTS

1. In the parable of the sower, some seed fell along . . . . . . and the birds came and ate it up. Some seed fell on . . . . . . and it sprouted quickly because . . . . . . Some seed fell among . . . . . . And some seed fell into good soil and the yield was . . . . . . fold . . . . . . fold even . . . . . . fold.
2. In the parable of the weeds, what did the servants want to do when they saw the weeds sprouting?
3. What did the master say to their idea?
4. What happened when the mustard seed was fully grown?
5. How much flour did the woman use with her yeast?
6. What did the man who found the treasure hidden in the field do?
7. How did he feel?
8. What did the merchant have to give up in order to have the pearl?
9. What do fishermen do with worthless fish?
10. Who will separate the evil people from the good?

2. THE TEACHING ABOUT THE KINGDOM

The evangelists give us an idealised picture of Jesus getting into a boat and pushing off a little way from shore, using the boat as a floating pulpit whence he could address the crowds on the shore. It is, of course, unlikely that he told all of these stories at a sitting. They have been grouped together in this way by the gospel writers.

In the church of St Leonard, St Leonard's-on-Sea, Sussex, the pulpit is a Galilean fisherman's boat. It was specially made and imported, under enormous difficulties soon after the Second World War to replace the traditional pulpit which had been destroyed during the war. From the boat, week by week, the word of God is preached in the same way that Jesus taught from a boat on the Sea of Galilee.

(a) PARABLE OF THE SOWER
Matt. 13.1 – 23: Mark 4.1 – 9: Luke 8.4 – 8

This is a good example of a parable which probably began life with one main message but which was afterwards given an allegorical interpretation (See Unit 14.1 (c) and (d)).
Jesus used the ordinary farming knowledge of his audience to talk about the growth of his own ministry. The sower sowed 'broadcast' i.e. he threw the seed in wide sweeping movements across his fields. *After* the seed was sown it was ploughed in, so the farmer was not being unduly careless by throwing the seed over the path. All would be ploughed and the path retrodden later. The soil in Galilee is shallow with limestone rock not far below the surface and the farmer knew that much of the seed he sowed would be wasted.
In Matthew verse 9 Jesus makes a characteristic remark — 'He who has ears to hear, let him hear' (RSV) i.e. 'Think it out for yourself.'
What was the 'single point' in this case which a true parable makes? How were the crowd to 'hear' i.e. 'understand' the story? The most obvious point is the contrast between the amount of seed sown and the great variance in yield. Jesus would have been applying this thought to his own ministry. Of the many thousands who heard him only some would understand and respond to what he was saying. To put it in modern terms, a teacher is sowing 'seeds of knowledge' all day long but look at the difference in examination results at the end of the year! You can see how this story would have a different meaning for teacher and pupils. To the teacher it might well speak encouragingly of the need to keep sowing in the knowledge that something will take root somewhere. To the students it may speak of their own part in learning. Are they the 'in-one-ear-out-the-other' kind i.e. where the birds came and devoured the seed? Or are they full of enthusiasm at first but without staying-power i.e. shallow soil? Or do they allow themselves to be distracted by outside pleasures or cares i.e. like seed choked by thorns?
So we find in Matthew verses 10–23 Jesus giving an allegorical interpretation of this parable to his own disciples. 'To you it has been given to know the secrets of the kingdom of heaven' (v.11). As they respond they will understand more and more.

People will frequently fail to understand the disciples' message but they must remember that some harvest is assured even though much of their work will seem to be failure. Their job is to keep sowing.

(b) PARABLE OF THE DARNEL (WEEDS)
Matt. 13.24 – 30

This is another example of a story which at first is a straightforward parable with one main point but which later (vv. 36 – 43) is given an allegorical interpretation. Before the days of selective weedkillers, it was a common sight around harvest time to see fields of corn speckled with poppies and cornflowers and big daisies. (Nowadays crops can be chemically sprayed before these weeds gain ground for, attractive though they appear, they are a nuisance to the farmer.) It was some such picture that Jesus had in mind in this story. The farmer has sown good seed. Where have the weeds come from? An enemy has been at work! The servants want to pull up the weeds but the farmer says 'No; lest in gathering the weeds you root up the wheat along with them' (v. 29). Wait till harvest and then they can be separated. You need to be aware that, in the Bible, imagery of harvest and the separation of good from bad refers to judgement. In other words, this story tells us to leave judgement to God. He will separate the good from the bad, the fruitful from the unfruitful, when his kingdom has fully come. It is not for human beings to decide who is 'righteous' and who is 'unrighteous'. If they do, they will only harm themselves. Be careful in the explanation (vv. 42–43) that you do not confuse imagery with fact. Jesus does *not* say that good people will turn into twinkling stars and bad people will burn in everlasting fires!

• ***GEHENNA***

The idea of everlasting flames for the wicked is associated with Gehenna. This was the rubbish dump west of Jerusalem. It was a place of evil associations, children at one time having been sacrificed there to the pagan god Moloch. Because it was a rubbish dump, fire was constantly burning there. Because it was outside the holy city, Jerusalem, it became a popular image for a place cut off from God, whose presence was with his people in the holy city. In Jewish imagination, therefore, the things associated with a rubbish dump — everlasting fire and worms — became associated with being cut off from God, an inevitable experience for those who constantly and knowingly turn their backs on him.

(c) PARABLE OF THE MUSTARD SEED
Matt. 13.31 – 32: Mark 4.30 – 32: Luke 13.18 – 19

The mustard seed, although tiny, is not quite the smallest of the seeds. On the shores of the Sea of Galilee it will growth to a height of about three and a half metres. So the theme of this parable is the great growth which can come from tiny beginnings.
For the disciples of Jesus it must have spoken of the apparently insignificant beginnings of the kingdom of God in the small community of those who responded to the preaching of John the Baptist and Jesus himself, and of the hoped-for greatness of its expected completion when even the Gentiles would be brought into it.

(d) PARABLE OF THE LEAVEN (YEAST)
Matt. 13.33: Luke 13.20 – 21

Another story of small beginnings and great endings but this time using the daily experience of housewives. If you have ever made bread you will be aware of the transforming power of a small quantity of yeast in a large lump of dough. Notice that the woman 'hides' the leaven in the flour. The beginnings of the kingdom of God are similarly hidden in the society to which Jesus' listeners belonged. They were unaware of it but already the transforming power of God was at work.

(e) PARABLE OF THE SEED GROWING SECRETLY Mark 4.26 – 29

When you sow seeds it is inadvisable to keep digging them up to see how they are growing! Similarly the farmer, once he has sown the seed, gets on with living and leaves the outcome to God. Were the disciples becoming impatient because there was no dramatic response to the ministry of Jesus? We know that at least one of them was a member of the Zealot party which was committed to the overthrow of the Roman government.

CHECK YOUR UNDERSTANDING

1. *What single main point do you think is intended in the parable of the sower?*
2. *Give an account of the allegorical interpretation of this parable.*
3. *Explain the meaning of the parable of the weeds.*
4. *Explain how the imagery of flames became attached to the idea of hell.*
5. *What meaning does the Bible give to the imagery of harvest?*
6. *What is the significance of birds coming to roost in the fully grown mustard plant?*
7. *Explain the meaning of the parable of the leaven.*
8. *What is there in common between these two parables?*
9. *What is there in common between the parables of the hidden treasure and the pearl of great price?*
10. *In what way do they differ?*

(f) PARABLE OF THE TREASURE HIDDEN IN THE FIELD Matt. 13.44

In a country which suffered frequent invasions, it was not uncommon for people to bury valuables before evacuating in the face of an invader. Not surprisingly they sometimes did not return or, if they did, could no longer identify the spot where they had hidden their treasure.
Here is a man who comes across such buried treasure and is so overjoyed that he rushes off to sell all he has in order to buy the field. Similarly the kingdom of God lies hidden and the man who finds it will need to sacrifice everything to obtain it, but his joy will be great.

(g) PARABLE OF THE PEARL OF GREAT PRICE Matt. 13.45–46

This parable forms a pair with the previous one. This time the man who finds the pearl is a merchant going about his ordinary work. He was probably wealthy but he still had to sacrifice everything to obtain the pearl. Sacrifice is necessary but well worthwhile.

(h) PARABLE OF THE NET Matt. 13.47 – 50

Another parable of separating. Fish must be sorted into those which can be eaten and those which cannot. It will be the same at the last judgement when the kingdom of God comes in power and is complete.

SUMMARY
From these parables we learn that:
(a) Response to the message of the kingdom will vary from total lack of interest to wholehearted participation.
(b) Those who respond will continue to live among those who do not but God will separate them when his kingdom has fully come.
(c) The beginnings of the kingdom are apparently insignificant but eventually it will embrace all nations.
(d) The transforming power of God is already at work although hidden.
(e) Growth must be left to God and man is not to worry about it.
(f) Those who join the kingdom must be prepared to sacrifice everything but will find great joy.

WHAT DO YOU THINK?
Look again at the above summary. Does it give an adequate picture of Jesus' teaching? What would you like to add to it?

Parables of Judgement

The parables to be considered in this unit are all about the coming of the kingdom of God and the judgement that its coming will bring. They sound a note of warning, telling of the need to be on the alert — to be watchful.

1. PARABLE OF THE TEN BRIDESMAIDS

Matt. 25.1 – 13

As usual, Jesus takes the ordinary experience of his listeners as the background to his story. A marriage has been arranged. The Bible frequently likens God's relationship with his people to a marriage (e.g. Hosea 2.16 – 20: Isaiah 62.4 – 5) and Jesus had spoken of himself as the bridegroom (Mark 2.19 – 20 Unit 10.3). In this story contemporary wedding customs are used as the framework for teaching. The bridegroom would go in procession to the bride's house. Then, accompanied by bridesmaids, both bride and bridegroom would return to the bridegroom's house where the ceremony would take place to be followed by a celebration with friends. READ THE TEXT.

As usual several interpretations are possible:

(a) The one main point seems to concern the necessity to be prepared.

(b) The emphasis can be put on the need for each *individual* to be responsible for himself. No one can rely on the good works of others to gain admittance to the Messianic banquet.

(c) Oil is a symbol of repentance and it is possible that a distinction is being made between those who have shown repentance as part of their preparation and those who have not.

(d) Notice that the parable ends with one of Jesus' characteristic pronouncements, 'Be on your guard then, because you do not know the day or the hour.' (v.13)

Remember with all the parables that the story will speak in different ways to different individuals at different times. These are suggestions only, not once and for all interpretations.

CHECK YOUR UNDERSTANDING

1. *In the parable of the bridesmaids, what is the significance of the marriage feast?*
2. *Suggest one main point made by Jesus in this parable.*
3. *To what is Jesus referring when he says 'you do not know the day or the hour?*

2. PARABLE OF THE TALENTS (GNB THREE SERVANTS)

Matt. 25.14 – 30: Luke 19.11 – 27

This parable explains more fully what is meant by being watchful. It is not a matter of sitting idly waiting. Jesus shows that being prepared for God's coming involves activity. A slave belonged to his master and any work the slave might do was done for his master's benefit, not his own.

A talent was a coin. Our modern saying about 'using one's talents' is a metaphor derived from this particular parable. Everybody has some talents although some are given more than others. However, if we fail to *use* the talents we have been given, we *lose* them. Musicians, for example, know that daily practice is essential however great their gift for music. Even a world famous pianist will have to practise daily and, if he doesn't, his public will soon notice the deterioration. Notice in this parable that the reward for loyal service is greater responsibility, not a rest from work.

Translated into religious terms, Christians would say that whatever talents they have been given are to be used in God's service, not hidden away. As they are used they will grow. St Luke's version of this parable, although similar in meaning, differs in

Vladimir Ashkenazy at the piano. If we do not use *talents we* lose *them.*

detail: e.g. the servants are all given the same amount at the beginning although the profit each makes varies as it does in St Matthew's account. *Make sure of the details in whichever version you are studying.*

3. PARABLE OF THE SHEEP AND THE GOATS

Matt. 25.31 – 46

This third and final parable of judgement is another story about separating the good from the bad. Can you remember two others? Look in Matthew 13 (Unit 16).

Sheep and goats grazed together in Palestine but had to be separated at night because goats needed to be kept warm. They were not as valuable as sheep — notice that the sheep are put on the right hand, the place of honour.

There are three points in the teaching to notice:

(a) It is deeds not words which count. The righteous are rewarded because they have helped to provide basic necessities for their fellow men.

(b) Jesus identified himself with the poor and needy. 'Whenever you refused to help one of these least important ones, you refused to help me.' (v.45 GNB)

(c) Neither the righteous nor the unrighteous were aware of serving, or failing to serve, the king.

This parable of the sheep and the goats is frequently quoted by Mother Teresa of Calcutta. It is at the root of her own work. As she tends a dying Hindu, rescues a newborn child from a dustbin or does any of the boring, backbreaking chores which her work requires, she is consciously serving Christ who is present in the outcast.

TEST YOURSELF ON FACTS

1. In what way were five bridesmaids foolish?
2. What did the wise ones say to them?
3. In the parable of the talents, what did the master do before he went on his journey?
4. What did each of the servants achieve?
5. What did the third servant say to his master on his return?
6. What did the master do?
7. In the parable of the sheep and the goats, list six things which the righteous had done.
8. What did the king say to the unrighteous?
9. Why did they feel unjustly treated?
10. Whom had they failed to serve?

WHAT DO YOU THINK?

1. The first Christians expected the second coming to happen soon. What effect would you expect this to have on the way they lived their lives?
   Look up 2 Thess. 3.6 – 12. This was St Paul's way of dealing with one group who were content to spend the waiting period in idleness. What connection can you see with the servants in the parable?
2. Look up the letter of James 2.14 – 26. How does this relate to the Parable of the Sheep and the Goats? Which do you think is the more effective way of teaching — parable or letter?

Sermon on the Mount Matt. 5

1. INTRODUCTION Matt. 5.1 – 2

The Sermon on the Mount is a handbook of Christian behaviour. The material in it is drawn from Q (Unit 2.1(b)) but St Matthew collects the sayings together in one long sermon. This is a literary device; it is unlikely that Jesus delivered it all at once on a single occasion.

There are three points to notice about the introduction:

(a) Jesus went up on the *mountain*. For Jews the mountain was the place where God spoke. Moses had gone up Mount Sinai to converse with God and had returned with the ten commandments as guidelines for living which he gave to the people of Israel. (Exod. 19 and 20).
Now Jesus, the leader of the new people of God, goes up the mountain to deliver teaching on how the new people of God are to live. St Matthew is interested in the symbolism not the geography.

(b) Jesus *sat down*. This was a sign that a rabbi was about to deliver important teaching. Remember that sermons in synagogues were delivered seated (Unit 11.4) i.e. this is not to be regarded as general advice given in passing but rather as the official teaching of Jesus.

(c) Jesus is speaking to *disciples* who have been learning from him about the nature of the kingdom and they would understand the demands he was making whereas they might seem impractical to other people.

2. THE BEATITUDES Matt. 5.3 – 10

Most mysterious of all are the eight sayings set at the opening of the sermon which summarise the rest of it. Known as the 'Beatitudes', they turn upside down the world's idea of happiness and startle by the raw and striking contradictions they contain.

You will find it helpful to learn the Beatitudes by heart. There are two parts to each of them — a statement of who is blessed followed by a statement of God's gift to the people concerned. Each begins 'Blessed are . .' (hence the name 'Beatitude' from the Latin '*beatus*' = 'blessed'). It is a very strong word — 'What bliss for those . . .' This blessedness is a deep inner happiness which nothing can touch.

(a) (i) *Blessed are the poor in spirit.* Matt. 5.3 (RSV)
'Happy are you poor', says St Luke and the word used means 'destitute', 'down and out'. Such a person has no influence in the world but may still be a person of integrity and may still hang on to his trust in God. There is a long tradition in the Old Testament of honouring such a person.
The New English Bible perhaps helps us understand better with the translation 'Happy are those who *know their need of God*.' Until a person is aware of his need, God cannot help him without denying him freewill. In Unit 10.2 it was suggested that a doctor can only help someone who is aware that he is ill and who seeks a cure. The same is true of a relationship with God. People are free to ignore him but, turning to him in need, the disciple is blessed because he has recognised his need.
(ii) *For theirs is the kingdom of heaven*
Remember that the 'kingdom of heaven' and the 'kingdom of God' are synonymous (Unit 16.1). A person becomes part of the kingdom of God when he accepts God as his king and lives according to his will. Doing so shows that he knows his need of God i.e. that he is in fact 'poor in spirit'.

(b) (i) *Blessed are those who mourn* Matt. 5.4
Surely not? How can it be blissful to have a broken heart? The experience of grief can never

TEXT QUIZ

1. Complete the following:
   Blessed are the poor . . . . . for theirs is . . . . . .
   Blessed are those who mourn, for they shall be . . . . .
   blessed are . . . . . for they shall inherit the earth.
   Blessed are those who hunger and thirst for . . . . . for they shall be . . . . .
   Blessed are the merciful for they . . . . .
   Blessed are . . . . . for they shall see God.
   blessed are . . . . . for they shall be called sons of God.
   Blessed are those . . . . . for theirs is the kingdom of heaven.
2. Jesus did not come to abolish the law of Moses but to . . . . . it.
3. Jesus says that . . . . . is as serious as murder.
4. What does Jesus teach about divorce, according to St Matthew's Gospel?
5. Give four examples used by Jesus of situations in which disciples might confront evil with kindness.

be a happy one and yet we know that we learn more through our bad experiences than through our happy ones. To whom do you turn when troubles come? Almost invariably to someone who has experienced trouble and so will understand. There is no short cut. If we are to become rich human beings we shall have to suffer. So, to some extent, this Beatitude means exactly and uncompromisingly what it says. Grief can be a blessing because turning to God in sorrow or penitence will provide the experience and joy of being restored.

(ii) *for they shall be comforted*

The full, rich meaning of the word translated as 'comforted' goes far beyond the easygoing sense of cheering someone up. It means 'make strong'. The teaching is that when a person turns to God in sorrow, God does indeed cheer him up but, beyond that, he makes him strong by restoring him and giving him his own strength to do his work.

(c) (i) *Blessed are the meek* Matt. 5.5

Meekness is not a quality we admire in the twentieth century. The Greek word translated in this way was used to describe the attitude of a trained animal — alert for the slightest indication of his master's intentions. Think of the dressage events involving horses, or sheepdog trials — such animals are controlled and obedient. The same word is used to describe the man who is obedient and controlled in his attitude to God. The word is associated with strength, not weakness. It might be used of a king who behaves with gentleness when he could assert his authority; it might be used of a poor person obedient to God's will like Mary saying 'be it unto me according to thy word' (Luke 1.38). Above all, it is the attitude of Jesus himself in the Garden of Gethsemane, praying that he might be spared the suffering but yet saying 'Thy will be done'.

Lipica horses — alert for the slightest indication of their riders intentions.

His followers must aim at this strong yet gentle 'meekness'.

(ii) *for they shall inherit the earth*

God had promised the Israelites that he would give them the promised land — Palestine. They, in turn, were to obey him and trust him. 'The earth' may therefore be understood in the limited sense of the country of Palestine promised to Abraham, or in the deeper, spiritual sense of the fullness of life promised by God to those who trust and obey him.

(d) (i) *Blessed are those who hunger and thirst for righteousness* Matt. 5.6

i.e. happy are the *wholehearted*. There must be no half measures. The desire for righteousness needs to be as intense as the desire of the starving for food. St Luke reverses the saying 'Woe to you that are full! for you shall hunger' (Luke 6.25). A person who is satisfied with himself will make no effort.

What is the righteousness which is to be sought so whole-heartedly? Nothing less than having a right relationship with God. Jews expressed this idea through the metaphor of a banquet to which men would be invited. God's people would always long for this great feast — not for the food itself but to be in the presence of the host.

(ii) *they shall be satisfied*

The Greek word used is very colloquial. It really means God will stuff them so full they could not possibly want anything more. All man's longings for God will be totally satisfied.

(e) (i) *Blessed are the merciful* Matt. 5.7

The merciful man is the man who has the same attitude to his fellow men that God has. He puts their needs before his own and tries to see life through the eyes of the person he is helping. The Christian sees the supreme example of God's mercy in the Incarnation.

(ii) *for they shall obtain mercy*

The man who is merciful in his judgements is growing more like God; the unmerciful man is growing further away from him. This is not a threat or punishment imposed from outside but the inevitable consequence of personal choices which make a person more or less like God. The merciful man, growing closer to God, is warmed by God's own mercy.

(f) (i) *Blessed are the pure in heart* Matt. 5.8

The person who is pure in heart is the person whose motives are unmixed. Jesus had said that purity was not a question of rituals, or refraining from eating certain foods (Mark

7.14 – 23) Unit 11.1 (c)) but of motives. Even generous actions can be motivated by pride, self-satisfaction. Do I make the donation to charity because I am 'merciful' and able to identify with those in need, or am I more concerned to be *seen* to do the right thing? Few people can say, hand on heart, that their motives are always pure.

(ii) *for they shall see God*

This would startle hearers because the Jewish scriptures regard seeing God as a terrible thing — 'There shall no man see me and live' (Exod. 33.20) and yet the servant was honoured to stand in the presence of the king. So, it is not a question of seeing God literally but rather of growing to understand, of coming to love him and so of being with him.

(g) (i) *Blessed are the peacemakers* Matt. 5.9

Notice that the blessed are peace *makers* rather than just peace *lovers*. We all love peace but it is often easier to sit back than to make the effort to restore right relations. This is not just a question of summit meetings between world powers; it involves everyone in the hurly-burly of everyday relationships with each other. The Hebrew word for peace, 'Shalom', means inward peace and fellowship as well as outward prosperity. Peace is much more than merely absence of war.

God's own peace is a positive active peace which the blessed transmit to others.

(ii) *for they shall be called sons of God*

Those who do God's work will be God's own children.

(h) (i) *Blessed are those who are persecuted for righteousness' sake* Matt. 5.10

Christians have been persecuted in many periods of history and have taken heart that Jesus had told them that it would be so. People who acknowledge a king over and above their worldy king would always seem to pose a political threat. When it became compulsory in the Roman Empire to worship Caesar as a god, Christians refused and were persecuted.

The blessedness of that persecution lies in the fact that it shows that the persecuted are being taken seriously. Nobody bothers to notice the weak. The more they were persecuted the more Christianity flourished and Tertullian was to say 'the blood of the martyrs is the seed of the Church'. It is still the same in the modern world.

3. SALT AND LIGHT

Matt. 5.13 – 16: Mark 9.50: Luke 14.34 – 35

(a) The disciples are to be salt to the world — another puzzling metaphor. Think of the uses of salt:

(i) it cleans and purifies
(ii) it preserves
(iii) it enhances flavour

Such is to be the role of the disciple in making the world acceptable to God. Furthermore if the disciple loses his enthusiasm and devotion, he will be as useless as tasteless salt.

(b) The disciples are to be like light in a dark place. The contrast between light and darkness is a favourite biblical symbol. Imagine a dark room. The light must not be hidden away but must be put in a position where it will shed its light on the surrounding darkness.

The light of Christ's teaching is to be shown in the *works* rather than the *words* of the disciples and these works will be done to the glory of God rather than the glorification of his servants.

4. JESUS AND THE LAW

Jesus goes on to say to his disciples 'You will be able to enter the Kingdom of heaven only if you are more faithful than the teachers of the law and the Pharisees in doing what God requires (Matt. 5.20 GNB). His teaching is to be no soft option. Jesus did not come to do away with the Law but to show the deep meaning in God's original intention which had been lost through turning God's Law into hundreds of man-made regulations. The rest of the chapter develops this idea by considering five examples of the Law. Each is introduced by the formula 'You have heard that it was said . . .' but I say unto you . . .'

(a) MURDER AND ANGER Matt. 5.21 – 25

Jesus first considers the sixth commandment (Exod. 20.13). Murder was a punishable offence but Jesus says that if his disciples are even angry in their hearts with a brother they have broken this commandment. Jesus is giving an inward, spiritual interpretation to the Law.

Not only is the disciple to avoid anger and using insulting language but he is also to take steps to remove the causes of anger felt by another toward himself. This may well be more difficult. Taking the initiative to make peace when one is in the wrong requires humility and courage as there is no guarantee that one's approach will not be rejected. Murder begins from anger so anger is just as serious a sin.

(b) ADULTERY AND LUST Matt. 5.27 – 30

Next Jesus considers the seventh commandment which forbids adultery. Again Jesus applies an inward interpretation saying that adultery has been committed as soon as the wish to do so has been allowed to take root.

The amusing illustration of plucking out the eye or cutting off the hand which is leading one astray is

Jesus' way of telling his disciples that if this is their problem, they are to avoid situations where they are likely to sin.

TEACHING ABOUT DIVORCE

In verse 31 Jesus quotes Deut. 24.1 which appeared to allow a husband to divorce his wife more or less on demand but he goes on to say that this was not God's intention in the Law. There is more extended and possibly contradictory teaching about divorce in Mark 10.1–10. Notice here the phrase (except on the ground of unchastity' (v.32). It is called St Matthew's 'exception clause' and it may well have been added by the early Church.

• *TEACHING ON DIVORCE*

Jewish teaching on divorce was based on Deut. 24.1. 'when a man has married a wife, but she does not win his favour because he finds something shameful in her . . .' (NEB) then he is allowed to divorce her.

Different rabbis gave different interpretations to this ground for divorce. The strictest, the school of Shammai, would only allow divorce on the ground of unchastity. The school of Hillel, on the other hand, interpreted the text far more liberally so that it could even include burning the husband's supper.

In Mark 10 Jesus was questioned about his own interpretation of the Law. Refusing to become involved in rabbinical argument, he goes back to God's original intention for marriage and quotes Gen. 1.27 where God created both male and female with the intention that they should have life-long companionship with each other and then says 'What God has joined together, man must not separate.' (Mark 10.9 NEB)

Later, in private, he expanded this teaching for the benefit of his disciples saying that 'whoever divorces his wife and marries another commits adultery against her.'

(Unusually for his times, Jesus further seems to admit the possibility that a wife might divorce her husband).

The 'exception clause' in Matt. 5.32 is usually thought to be the work of the early Church. Jesus was to give the apostles power to 'bind' and 'loose' i.e. to interpret the Law, and, in certain circumstances to make exceptions. This may well be an example of their doing so.

(c) TEACHING ABOUT OATHS Matt. 5.33–37

Jesus goes on to deal with a third example of how man-made rules had undermined God's original intention.

When people were making particularly solemn promises they were taken in God's name and were then regarded as completely binding. However, we have already seen (Unit 16.1) that God's name was so holy that Jews avoided uttering it, using instead things associated with him such as 'heaven' or 'Jerusalem'. Over the years, oaths sworn by these less holy symbols came to be regarded as less binding. The original intention had been to encourage people to be honest in their dealings with each other. Man-made regulations were defeating this aim. Jesus tells his disciples they are not to swear at all — 'Plain "yes" or "no" is all you need to say' (NEB). The disciples' word should be trustworthy.

Quakers (members of the Society of Friends) have always strictly kept to this teaching and refuse to take an oath in court.

(d) RETALIATION AND NON-RESISTANCE

Matt. 5.38–42: Luke 6.29–30

In ancient times, when a member of one tribe was injured by a member of another, there was no limit to revenge as one side tried to get even with the other. So the Law of Moses, 'An eye for an eye and a tooth for a tooth', (Exod. 21.24: Lev. 24.20: Deut. 19.21) was a great step forward in its day through limiting the extent of revenge. If someone knocked out one of your teeth you could knock out one of his — but *only* one! Gradually, of course, fines came to take the place of this literal requirement. The disciples however, are children of God and no father wants fighting in the family. They are to be peace makers and are not to return evil for evil. Instead they are to absorb it and change it into love. If they are attacked they are not to retaliate. If their coat (a long under-garment with sleeves) is taken from them (which was allowed as a fine or a pledge) they are to offer their cloak (the warm outer garment) as well. Soldiers in the occupying Roman army were allowed to force passers-by to carry things for them although the distance was limited to one Roman mile. If the disciple finds himself a victim in this position, he is not merely to go the one mile required by law but is also to travel gladly a second mile — the first because he has to, the second to show love to his enemy. He is to give to beggars and to be a willing lender rather than clinging to his personal possessions.

(e) LOVE YOUR ENEMIES

Matt. 5.43–48: Luke 6.27–28 and 32–36

The Jews were not told in their Law to hate their enemies although we have seen that it allowed considerable limitation to the understanding of who was a neighbour.

Jesus says that his followers should have no enemies since the people they find difficult are

Mahatma Ghandi

Martin Luther King

also children of God and therefore brothers. There is no virtue in liking people who like us. The follower of Christ is taught that he must love his enemies. This does not mean that he needs to feel emotionally attracted to them. It does mean that he must treat them with the same care and concern that he would show to those he finds it easy to like. The whole of the new law can therefore be summarised in the one word 'Love'.

DISCUSSION TOPICS

1. *If God desires our welfare, why does he allow suffering? Do you agree that those who mourn are blessed?*
2. *Is it possible to be both tough and 'meek' in the sense in which the word is used in Matt. 5.5?*
3. *Portia in* The Merchant of Venice *says of mercy 'it is twice blessed: it blesseth him that gives and him that takes.' What did she mean? Does this agree with the fifth beatitude? Can you give examples either from your own experience or from history of people who have shown mercy?*
4. *How would you recognise the 'pure in heart'? Can you think of examples of people with this quality? Tell the rest of the class about them.*
5. *Is it ever right to be angry? What is meant by righteous indignation? In what circumstances might righteous indignation become* unrighteous?
6. *'The Church has the duty to uphold Christ's teaching on divorce but also the duty to show love to the victims of divorce.' In the light of this statement, do you consider people who have been divorced should be allowed to remarry in church?*
7. *Do you think it is possible to live up to Christ's teaching on non-violence? Remember that the world Jesus lived in was violent too. It is no use arguing that his way can only work if everybody adopts it. In our own century non-violence has been the attitude and the weapon of Martin Luther King and of Gandhi. Dr King was a Christian, Mahatma Gandhi a Hindu. If you do not know about their achievements, find out about them.*
8. *Does the Sermon on the Mount provide a case for unilateral disarmament?*

Sermon on the Mount Matt. 6 and 7

Jesus next goes on to consider three important religious practices and to give his disciples advice on how to engage in them.

1. ALMSGIVING Matt. 6.2 – 4

In a religion which paid as much attention to the keeping of rules as Judaism did, there was an ever-present danger of religious duties being undertaken for the wrong reasons. It is all too easy to make a great show of piety in order to impress other people. Jesus makes it quite clear to his followers that such behaviour is hypocritical and does no honour to God. So, when they give to the poor, his disciples are to do so in secret, not looking for any reward and certainly not making their gift with a flourish.

2. PRAYER Matt. 6.5 – 15: Luke 11.2 – 4

Similarly with prayer. There was a real temptation for religious people to stand up and make a great show of long prayers in the synagogues. Jesus' disciples are not to behave in this way but are told 'go into your room and shut the door' i.e. pray in private. 'The room' can be understood both literally and metaphorically i.e. it can mean 'shut distractions from your mind and turn to God'.

In verses 7–8 Jesus warns against long prayers full of empty words, saying God already knows of our needs before we tell him.

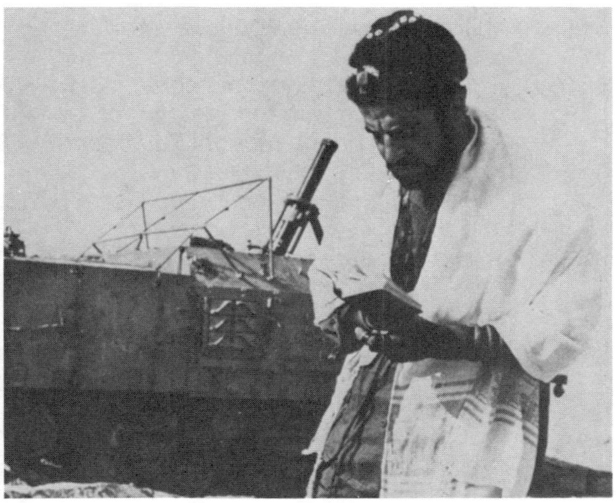

An Israeli soldier, from a heavy mortar unit, prays in the Sinai desert.

The Lord's Prayer Matt. 6.9 – 15: Luke 11.2 – 4

There are two versions of the Lord's prayer, one in Luke and the other in Matthew. St Matthew's version is the longer one so it seems likely that he expanded the basic prayer in 'Q', which was also used by St Luke, in order to make its meaning clearer.

Our Father

The disciples are to adopt Jesus' own way of addressing God, that of a child turning in trust to a loving father. Jesus uses the child's word 'Abba' (= 'Dad') rather than the formal religious word 'Abinu' and so transforms the relationship from one of formality, in which the person praying stands at a distance, into one of trust and confidence such as is found in the relaxed atmosphere within a loving family.

who art in heaven

a reminder of the greatness and majesty of God.

hallowed by thy name

Remember that, in the Bible, 'Name' = 'character/nature'. The disciple asks that God may always be reverenced as holy.

Thy kingdom come

Although the kingdom of God is already present in Jesus and, to some extent in the disciples, they are to pray that it will spread until God is accepted as king by all men.

Thy will be done on earth as it is in heaven

i.e. the kingdom will come when men are prepared to obey God.

Give us this day our daily bread

The disciple is to trust God for *basic* needs. He is not to ask for cake, nor for food for a week. Christians also see a deeper meaning in this clause based on a saying in the Fourth Gospel — 'I AM the Bread of Life' (John 6.35) so the Christian is also asking to be fed day by day with the life of Christ himself.

And forgive us our debts As we also have forgiven our debtors.

St Luke uses the word 'sins' but the meaning is similar. God's forgiveness cannot be received unless the disciple is prepared to forgive those who have wronged him (Look again at Matt. 5.23 – 24). This clause is regarded as so important that St Matthew repeats its teaching in verses 14 – 15.

And lead us not into temptation

God does not tempt. The disciple is asking for his protection from trials which might be too severe for him.

But deliver us from evil (or 'the evil one')

i.e. the disciple is to trust God to save him from being overwhelmed by the evil which surrounds him.

You will notice that the text does not include the usual doxology 'for thine is the kingdom . . .' This is a later addition which was used by early Christians when they prayed together and was not part of the original prayer found in the gospels.

3. FASTING

Fasting is a form of self-discipline used to reinforce prayer. Jesus' disciples had been criticised for *not* fasting (Mark 2.18 – 22 Unit 10.3). Jesus says, as with almsgiving and prayer, it is something between the individual and God and should be practised in private. In fact the disciple should take steps to throw people off the scent by anointing his head and washing his face as though he were full of joy and ready to celebrate. The fasting is then a true offering to God alone.

4. TRUE WEALTH Matt. 6.19 – 24

Nowadays people rate very highly the acquisition of material possessions particularly money because of the things it can buy. The Jews did this too and regarded money as a sign of God's favour. It made easier the good works on which they believed salvation to depend. Jesus questioned this whole attitude because he saw that money created as many problems as it solved. His disciples were to have their eyes on 'treasure in heaven', God's kingdom (*not* pie in the sky). He uses three saying to make his point:

(a) Where your treasure is, there will your heart be also.' If the disciple sets his heart on material things, he will put his energies into acquiring more of them. If, on the contrary, his heart is set on the coming of God's kingdom, he will find riches there — and those riches will go with him beyond the grave.

(b) 'the eye is the lamp of the body . . .'
If the disciple 'sees things straight' i.e. gets his priorities right, he will find his life filled with the light of God's own life. If, however, he is blinded by materialism, he will really be feeling his way through a shadowy, basically unsatisfying existence.

(c) 'No man can serve two masters . . .'
Mammon is an Aramaic word meaning 'material things'. The disciple cannot be chasing after money and serving God at the same time. He has to choose.

5. ANXIETY Matt. 6.25 – 34

Furthermore nothing is to be gained by worrying. This famous passage is an excellent example of Jesus' use of exaggeration to make his point. He is encouraging his followers to be care*free* not care*less*. Of course it is necessary to plan what we are going to eat for supper and make sure we have a warm winter coat before the snow arrives but to worry endlessly about these things shows lack of faith. The disciples' purpose in life needs to be the service of God and they are to trust him to provide the basic necessities.
Finally, take one day at a time. Nothing can be done about tomorrow's worries today so don't meet trouble halfway.

6. JUDGING AND ASKING

Matt. 7.1 – 12: Mark 4.24: Luke 6.37 – 42; 11.9 – 13

Why do we criticise each other? Usually because it makes us feel superior. This is pride. Jesus warns his disciples against judging other people. Only God can judge as only God knows all the circumstances. Instead of making much of the sins of others, disciples need to make the effort to become aware of their own. Jesus, the carpenter, uses a vivid image taken from his own trade to

DISCUSSION TOPICS

1. *If God already knows our needs, why pray?*
2. *Is the poster about a sponsored fast in accordance with the teaching of the Sermon on the Mount? You need to consider the reason for the sponsoring, the reason for the fast and the motives of all concerned.*
3. *Would you agree that we all worry too much? Is Jesus' teaching about anxiety realistic in the twentieth century?*
4. *Jesus asks 'Ask and you will receive,' yet we have all at some time asked and* ***not*** *received. Look again at the section Matt. 7.7 – 12. Does the rest of the teaching offer any explanation of why we do not always receive what we ask for?*
5. *'Be ye perfect'. Since we are all bound to fail, should the standard be lowered? Give reasons.*

make his point. Why try to take a speck of sawdust out of your neighbour's eye when there is a great plank in your own? The disciple must set his own sin right first and then he will see more clearly to help his neighbour.

7. PEARLS BEFORE SWINE Matt. 7.6

This proverb interrupts the sequence of the arguments and it is not clear why St Matthew included it at this point. An allegorical interpretation might suggest that the 'pearl' of the gospel should not be offered to 'dogs', meaning Gentiles. It seems more probable however that Jesus is warning his disciples that there will always be people who will scoff at his teaching. In the same way that they would not give holy things to dogs or allow pigs (unclean animals to the Jews) to trample on pearls, they should not attempt to teach people who are not ready to listen seriously to the precious things of God.

8. MORE ABOUT PRAYER Matt. 7.7 – 11

Disciples are to keep asking God for their needs. An ordinary human father would not mock his son by offering him a stone when he asks for bread or a snake when he asks for a fish. 'How much more, then, will your Father in heaven give good things to those who ask him.' (v.11 GNB)

9. THE GOLDEN RULE Matt. 7.12

The idea of treating others as we would like them to treat us occurs in a number of religions and Jesus is quoting a view which was common teaching among the rabbis.

10. TWO WAYS
Matt. 7.13 – 23: Luke 13.24 – 27 and 6.43 – 44

There are two ways of living. One leads to eternal life and the other to destruction. Jesus make three points:

(a) The way of life is narrow. It is a struggle to find it. There is to be no easy strolling in to the kingdom of God.
(b) His disciples must beware of false teaching. How are they to know true teaching from false? By noting its effect in the lives of those who follow it. Those who follow God's teaching are like trees bearing good fruit. St Paul listed these 'fruits of the Spirit' as 'love, joy, peace, patience, kindness, goodness, faithfulness, humility and self-control.' (Gal. 5.22 GNB)
(c) It is actions, not words which count (compare the parable of the sheep and the goats in Matt. 25.31–46 Unit 17.3(a)).

11. PARABLE OF THE TWO FOUNDATIONS

The Sermon on the Mount ends with a simple story. The disciples can build their lives on the rock-like foundation of Christ's teaching or they can be like the man who builds on sand. In that case they must not be surprised if their building does not withstand the storms of life.

12. CONCLUSIONS

What are we to make of this most quoted of Christian documents? Four things need to be said:

(a) It sets an impossible standard — 'Be ye perfect' — which is beyond Man's efforts to attain but that is no excuse for not trying. The disciple will often fail and then he will have to ask for forgiveness which will draw him closer to God. As he draws closer to God he will gradually, very gradually, be changed and so *through failure he is made strong*. (Matt. 5.4)
(b) It is not a set of rules to be obeyed in all circumstances but rather a frame of reference setting out principles by which to live.
(c) It is addressed to disciples, people who are already committed to Christ. Their experience of Jesus himself makes sense of the paradoxes (= apparently absurd or contradictory statements) found in the teaching, especially of the Beatitudes. They have seen the truth of them in Jesus himself.
(d) It does not set out a programme of reforms for society at large but offers a way of changing the hearts and minds of men — the place where the kingdom of God eventually takes root.

TEXT QUIZ

1. What does Jesus say about almsgiving?
2. Where does Jesus say his disciples should go to pray?
3. What does Jesus teach about fasting?
4. What advice does Jesus give to help curb anxiety?
5. How are the disciples to recognise false prophets?
6. 'Not everyone who calls me "Lord, Lord" will enter the kingdom of heaven, but only those who . . .' — What?

Use of Wealth

First remind yourself of what Jesus said about real wealth in the Sermon on the Mount (Matt. 6.19 – 24 Unit 19.4). Notice that he does not say that money is evil in itself. It was St Paul who wrote that *'Love* of money is the root of all evil' (1 Tim. 6.10 NEB), although his view was probably a fair reflection of the attitude of Jesus himself.

We know that Jews regarded wealth as a blessing from God but this attitude presupposes that the money is going to be used for God's work and to God's glory. Jesus knew that the possession of wealth could be a danger in two ways:

(a) It could be used for *self*-glorification making a person self-centred.

(b) Its possession could become an end in itself making the rich man selfish, indifferent to the needs of others and dependent on his money for security rather than placing his trust in God.

In this Unit we shall look at three encounters Jesus had with real people and at three parables which deal with the question of money.

1. THE RICH YOUNG RULER

Mark 10.17 – 30: Matt. 19.16 – 30: Luke 18.18 – 30

A rich man comes to Jesus and asks him what he must do to receive eternal life. He seems to think that eternal life is a prize to be won by hard work — an attitude which was hardly surprising bearing in mind the Jewish emphasis on keeping the Law. Jesus rebukes his effusiveness with 'Why do you call me good?' and reminds him of the commandments which set out our duty to our neighbour (if you are not familiar with them, check them in Exod. 20). Astonishingly, the young man is able to say that he has kept these laws all his life. Yet he is aware that keeping to the rules has not brought him closer to God; otherwise he would not have asked the question.

Only St Mark gives us the human detail that Jesus looked straight at him *with love*. Jesus recognises that goodness is a positive, active quality rather than merely an absence of weakness. Keeping to the Law, although good in itself, is not enough. The young man needs a challenge. Jesus puts his finger on the man's weakness — 'Go and sell all you have and give the money to the poor, and you will have riches in heaven; then come and follow me.' (GNB)

He realises that the barrier which separates the man from God is his money. He relies on his money for his security rather than relying on God. Doubtless he would have liked to 'give Jesus a trial', to become a disciple for a time, as long as he had his money to fall back on if life with Jesus did not work out as he hoped. But he would never find out what the life of the Kingdom was like by sticking one toe into the water. He needed to jump in at the deep end in the faith that he would not sink. The wholeheartedness taught in the Beatitudes is basic. So he turned sadly away — and Jesus *let him go*.

Notice the teaching which follows:

(a) Jesus says 'How hard it will be for rich people to enter the kingdom of God' (Mark, verse 23). The disciples are shocked so Jesus expands what he has said.

(b) Mark verse 27 is *very* important. People are saved not by their own efforts but purely through the generous love of God.

(c) The story of the camel and the needle-eye tells of the need for getting rid of anything which hinders becoming citizens of the kingdom of God. A needle-eye was a narrow entrance through the walls of Jerusalem through which a laden camel could not pass without first unloading.
Similarly those who enter the kingdom must do some unloading.

(d) Even Peter has not yet grasped the lesson. He thinks the twelve must be 'one up' on everyone else because they have followed Jesus and will surely therefore be rewarded. There is wry humour in Jesus' reply in Mark verses 29 – 30. He agrees the reward will be great — 'a hundred times more houses, brothers, sisters, mothers, children and fields — and persecutions as well'!

2. ZACCHAEUS Luke 19.1 – 9

By contrast St Luke tells us the story of a man who was rich in material things but aware of his spiritual poverty. His encounter with Jesus changed his whole life and attitude to money. Zacchaeus was a chief tax collector and therefore unpopular. He must have heard of Jesus and of his generous friendship for the outcasts of society so, when Jesus passes through Jericho, he is determined to see him

— so determined that he braves ridicule by shinning up a tree to get a better view. (The tree, incidentally, would not have been an English sycamore but a fig-mulberry tree.)
As Jesus passes he looks up and calls Zacchaeus by name. We may wonder how Jesus knew his name. Probably the crowds were jeering at him.
There are five things to notice in this story:
(a) Jesus' acceptance of those despised by orthodox Jews (v.5 'I must stay in your house today').
(b) The criticism of Jesus by the Jews (v.7 'This man has gone as a guest to the home of a sinner.')
(c) The joy felt by the sinner who knows himself to be accepted.
(d) The difference the friendship of Jesus makes. In this case Zacchaeus, without being asked, says he will repay the overcharged taxes four times over — an amount more than twice that required by the Law in the case of robbery.
So here is a story where the love of Jesus breaks through the barrier which money, gained by cheating, had erected between Zacchaeus and God and enabled the man to start a new life. No wonder Jesus said 'Salvation (= spiritual health) has come to this house today!' (GNB)

3. THE WIDOW'S MITE

Mark 12.41 – 44: Luke 21.1 – 4

The last story concerning real people and money centres on a poor widow rather than a wealthy person.
As he sits near the temple treasury watching people put money into the box, Jesus points out to his disciples that a poor widow who drops in two tiny coins has, in fact, made a greater offering to God than many of the wealthy who have given large sums which they could easily afford. The widow is making a real sacrifice — 'she, poor as she is, put in all she had — she gave all she had to live on.' (Mark v.44 GNB)
There is an added poignancy in St Mark's setting of this story at this point in his narrative. Jesus has come to Jerusalem to die. He too was soon to give 'all he had' — his life. So here we learn that offering large gifts which cost nothing is not real generosity. Real generosity is offering what genuinely costs us something.
Jesus also told several parables about the use of wealth.

TEST YOURSELF ON FACTS

1. How did the rich young ruler answer Jesus' question?
2. What comparison did Jesus use to show how hard it would be for a rich man to enter the kingdom of God?
3. What did Jesus say to Zacchaeus?
4. What did the crowds say?
5. What did Zacchaeus say?
6. What did Jesus say when he saw the widow putting two small coins into the treasury?
7. What did the rich fool plan to do when he had a good harvest?
8. What did Abraham reply to the rich man's request for Lazarus to take him some water?
9. How does the rich man hope to help his five brothers?
10. What does Abraham say to that request?

CHECK YOUR UNDERSTANDING

1. *What do you understand by 'eternal life'?*
2. *Why would the idea of riches as a barrier to discipleship have been hard for the disciples to accept?*
3. *What does Jesus mean by ''Salvation'' has come to this house today!'?*
4. *What lesson does the story of the rich fool teach?*
5. *What meanings do you see in the parable of the rich man and Lazarus?*

4. THE RICH FOOL Luke 12.13 – 21

One day Jesus was asked to settle a family quarrel over a will. Two brothers were unable to agree and one of them thought Jesus would find a way of restoring peace.
Instead, Jesus tells a story to show that *both* are in the wrong, because of their obsession with material things.
Notice that the rich farmer is totally self-centred. Count up how many times the words 'I' and 'my' occur in this story. His whole life is spent in amassing wealth. And what for? Just as he thinks he has enough stored away to enjoy himself for years, God speaks 'You fool!' He had done nothing with his money which was of any value in the sight of God.

5. THE RICH MAN AND LAZARUS

Luke 16.19 – 31

The rich man in this story is often known as Dives, which is the Latin word for 'rich'. The name Lazarus means 'Leper'. The story is based on a Jewish folk-tale to which Jesus gives a special twist and is not to be regarded as a geographical guide to the hereafter!
There is no suggestion that the rich man is wicked *because* he is rich nor that Lazarus is good *because* he is poor. It is the characters of the two which bring

A street party, Horley, to mark the Queen's Silver Jubilee.

about the reversal of their situations in the after-life.

The rich man had ignored human need and cannot plead that he did not know that Lazarus existed — he knew his name. His money had made him *self*-centred and had diminished him as a human being. Lazarus, on the other hand, had not become embittered by his painful experience and so is rewarded. Abraham was the founding father of the Jewish nation and was close to God so, sitting beside him at the feast in heaven means Lazarus has received a place of honour.

The twist in the tale comes at the end. The rich man asks for warning to be sent to his brothers so that they may be spared his horrible fate. He feels sure that an apparition from the dead would convince them of the need to mend their ways. Notice that he himself has not changed. He still regards Lazarus as a slave to do him service. But Abraham refuses. His brothers know the Law of Moses. If they are not convinced by that of the need to care for their fellow men, they will not be convinced even if someone should *rise from the dead*. Think of the impact of those words on first generation Christians who worshipped a recently risen Christ!

6. HOSPITALITY Luke 14.12 – 14

Another parable about the wise use of material things comes in a group of three stories about giving parties. Jesus had noticed how the guests at a supper were all trying to seize the places of honour for themselves and first of all tells a story about a man who had been made to look foolish when he had been displaced by someone more honourable. He then goes on to say that, when a man gives a party, he should not confine his guest list to those able to repay him but should invite the poor and needy as well. In other words his disciples should give gladly and freely without expecting returns. They will find happiness in doing so and will be rewarded by God.

7. SUMMARY

Jesus' teaching about wealth can be summarised thus:

(a) There is danger in man putting his trust in material possessions. True security lies in faith in God.
(b) Generosity involves personal sacrifice and a willingness to give without thought of any return.
(c) Wealth which is used for selfish purposes is valueless in God's eyes.
(d) Wealth is God's gift with which to do his will in this life and 'you can't take it with you'.

WHAT DO YOU THINK?

Can a Christian allow himself to become rich? Give reasons.

Albert Schweitzer tells us that it was the parable of the Rich Man and Lazarus which sent him to Africa — an example of the power of the gospel to speak in modern times. Find out about Schweitzer's work at Lambarene What is the connection with the parable?

Caesarea Philippi

We come now to a great turning point in the gospels. The incident at Caesarea Philippi is recorded exactly halfway through St Mark's Gospel. For eight chapters St Mark has recorded the actions of Jesus which should have indicated to anyone attuned to the Messianic expectation of the Jews that here was the Messiah himself. The evangelists have recorded his teaching — some of it, in parables, to people in general; some of it, in short pithy sayings or more extended 'sermons' for the ears of those closest to him. How much of it were they absorbing? Was what they saw and heard leading them to the realisation of the fact that Jesus was the Christ?

St Mark shows us that, shortly before this point, as far as the disciples were concerned the penny had still not dropped. Jesus had been trying without much success to help them 'see' the meaning of the feeding miracles. In Mark 8.17–18 he questions them closely. 'Have you no inkling yet? Do you still not understand?' (NEB) Patiently he draws plodding answers to his questions from them but still at the end has to say 'Do you still not understand?' Jesus must have known that time was running out as far as his own ministry was concerned. He would be leaving his work in the hands of this collection of twelve ordinary men. How could he help them realise the truth? Then Mark, alone of the evangelists, having shown the blindness of the disciples to the identity of Jesus, switches to the healing of a physically blind man.

1. THE BLIND MAN OF BETHSAIDA

Mark 8.22–26

Only St Mark draws out the significance of this story. He uses it as a pivot on which to turn to the next section of the Gospel.

Notice the details in the story:

(a) Jesus leads the blind man to a quiet place away from the village.
(b) He spits on his eyes (remember the healing of the deaf mute in Mark 7.31–37 Unit 13.2 (c)), lays hands on them and the man's sight begins to return.
(c) Jesus lays hands on his eyes a second time and completes the cure.
(d) The story ends with Jesus telling the man to keep quiet about what he has done (in line with the Messianic secret — see Unit 9.4 (d)).

Students frequently ask how a blind man was able to describe trees which they assume he had never seen. However, we are not told he had been blind from birth!

2. PETER'S CONFESSION OF FAITH

Mark 8.27–33: Matt. 16.13–23: Luke 9.18–22

Immediately St Mark goes straight into the story of the moment when the disciples at last 'see' i.e. recognise who Jesus really is.

Notice the parallels with the healing of the blind man:

(a) Jesus is away from the crowds alone with his disciples.
(b) He leads them *in two stages* to 'see' that he is the Messiah in the same way that he had healed the blind man in two stages.
(c) Once they have 'seen', he immediately instructs them to tell no one.

Students often wonder why Jesus did not make a

clear statement of his identity to his disciples. Why should it be necessary for them to struggle through to the answer for themselves in this way? Surely it must be for the same reason that students have to struggle through a mathematical problem for themselves. It would be easy enough for a teacher to do it for them but the very struggle makes the knowledge they gain their own. Up to a point everyone can pass examinations by memorising answers but, unless people learn to think for themselves, they will never be able to tackle fresh problems on their own with much hope of success. This was the point the disciples had reached. Quite soon now, although they did not realise it, they were going to have to face terrible troubles very much on their own. It was essential that they should have taken the knowledge that Jesus was the long-awaited Messiah right into the very core of their beings. The intellectual knowledge which might have been imparted by a straightforward statement would not be enough to sustain them in what they were about to face. The 'heart' knowledge which would come from working the question out for themselves would lead them along the path they would have to tread. Jesus is testing their understanding.

The first question Jesus asks, 'Who do men say I am?' starts their minds moving in the right direction. They are only too willing to tell him. There is kudos attached to being associated with someone so great.

The student is advised to switch to St Matthew's version of the incident at this point in Matt. 16.13–23 since he gives more detail than St Mark.

'Some say John the Baptist, others Elijah, others Jeremiah, or one of the prophets.' — all great men of Jewish history, very recent history in the case of John the Baptist.

Then — the second stage — 'who do you say I am?' As one might expect, it is Peter, the every-ready spokesman, who blurts out 'You are the Messiah, the Son of the living God.' He has 'arrived' and Jesus tells him that his understanding is a gift to him from God himself.

The next two verses in St Matthew's Gospel are interpreted in different ways by different sections of the Church:

(a) On the one hand some would say that Jesus was giving special authority to St Peter and that this authority has been passed on to all Peter's successors.

(b) On the other hand others believe that Jesus meant that the Church (= the body of people, *not* a building) would be founded on the kind of faith in Christ which Peter has just expressed.

Similarly Christians differ in their interpretation of 'binding' and 'loosing' conferred in verse 19.

(a) Some believe that Jesus was giving his own authority to forgive sins to Peter as leader of the Church.

(b) Others interpret this passage as meaning that Peter was being given authority to *interpret* rules in Christ's name. In the same way that Jewish scribes interpreted the Law for Jews, the disciples were to interpret the Law for Christians. We have already considered one example of their doing so in our consideration of the 'exception clause' in St Matthew's account of Christ's teaching on divorce (Matt. 5.31: Unit 18.4 (b)).

Finally Jesus gives his disciples strict instructions not to tell anyone that he is the Messiah. In view of the Jewish expectations of the Messiah (see Unit 6.1) this was clearly a necessary move. All three gospels tell us that, as soon as they acknowledged him as Messiah, Jesus immediately starts to teach his disciples that the Messiah must suffer.

TEST YOURSELF ON FACTS

1. What did Jesus do first to the blind man of Bethsaida?
2. What was the result?
3. What did Jesus do next?
4. What instruction did Jesus give him after healing him?
5. What did the disciples reply to the question 'Who do men say the Son of Man is?'
6. What did Jesus reply when Peter said 'You are the Messiah'?
7. How did Peter react when Jesus told his disciples he would have to suffer?
8. What did Jesus then say to Peter?

3. FIRST PREDICTION OF THE PASSION

Matt. 16.21–23: Mark 8.31–3: Luke 9.21–22

The word 'passion' means suffering. This is the first time that Jesus has mentioned a possible tragic end to his ministry. Will the disciples be able to accept it or will they abandon him?

In order to understand what happens, it is necessary to know that a suffering Messiah was a contradiction in terms for the Jews who believed that the Messiah would not have to endure even ordinary human suffering. This would cause great difficulty for the disciples. They would inevitably think either that they must be wrong in acknowledging Jesus as Messiah or that Jesus himself must be mistaken about the suffering. It is left to the irrepressible Peter to seize Jesus by the arm and say 'No, Lord, this shall never happen to you,' but he is sharply rebuked, 'Away with you, Satan.' (Revise Unit 6 on the Temptations.) From now onward the shadow of the cross falls over the narrative but, before Jesus finally sets his face towards Jerusalem and all that would happen there, one more transforming event occurs to help the disciples — the transfiguration, which will be considered in the next Unit.

CHECK YOUR UNDERSTANDING

1. *What connection do you see between the story of the healing of the blind man of Bethsaida and Peter's confession of faith?*
2. *Describe two different interpretations of 'on this rock I will build my church'.*
3. *Describe two different interpretations of 'loosing and binding'.*
4. *Why were the disciples bewildered by the first prediction of the Passion?*

WHAT DO YOU THINK?

Find out about similar experiences in the twentieth century when people are either converted to religion or see richer significance in it. People to investigate might include Cliff Richard, James Galway and C.S. Lewis.

One of a series of modern elmwood sculptures by Tom Preator in a Taunton church. The foreshortened perspective and upside-down effect emphasises the agony of Jesus and the theme of binding and loosing, symbolised by the rope, runs right through the series

Transfiguration

1. THE TRANSFIGURATION

Mark 9.2 – 13: Luke 9.28 – 36: Matt. 17.1 – 13

We have seen how the disciples were puzzled by the idea of a suffering Messiah. The next incident shows how they came to terms with it. Three of the disciples seem to have been closer to Jesus than the rest. This does not mean that he had favourites. Perhaps they were more sensitive to his teaching and more determined to learn all they could from their master. Whatever the reason, it is this 'inner circle', Peter, James and John, who go up the mountain with Jesus.

St Luke alone of the gospel writers tells us *why* they went up the mountain — to pray — and so provides a clue to help us understand what happened next. Remember the shock they had so recently received when Jesus had spoken about the suffering he must undergo. Not only were the disciples puzzled but they had a sense of a new seriousness and a fresh sense of urgency in Jesus himself. Small wonder that they wanted to pray. What happened? As Jesus prayed, his face and his clothes became dazzling white 'with a whiteness no bleacher on earth could equal' according to St Mark (9.3 NEB) who wants to leave us in no doubt that what they saw was beyond ordinary human experience. St Luke says that the disciples were at first asleep but all three Evangelists agree that the disciples were aware of this strange phenomenon. There are stories of a luminous glow surrounding saints when deep in prayer and it could be that the disciples saw something of the kind. But, in that case, what about Moses and Elijah? Were they *really* there, physically, in person, or were these three devout disciples being helped through prayer to 'see' Jesus in relation to these two key figures of Jewish history and faith? Moses represented the Law and Elijah the prophets — twin pillars of the Jewish religion. Seeing Jesus talking to them confirmed the disciples in their conviction that Jesus was of the highest spiritual importance and through the experience their questionings and doubts were answered. 'Then a cloud appeared' (verse 7) — in Jewish thought the appearance of the cloud (*shekinah*) symbolises the presence of God. In the days of the Exodus God had been present among his people in a pillar of cloud by day and of fire by night (e.g. Exod. 16.10: 19.9 and 16: 24.15 et al.) and a voice spoke from the cloud 'This is my Son, my Beloved, listen to him.' The words are so similar to those spoken at the Baptism of Jesus that we are bound to compare the two experiences. They were similar in three respects:

(a) Both are concerned to reveal Jesus as the Messiah. At his Baptism it was Jesus who received reassurance about his mission. At the Transfiguration the disciples are given the reassurance about him that they need.

(b) In both incidents the revelation comes through a vision and a voice.

(c) The words spoken by the voice are almost identical.

In the middle of it all Peter, although terrified by such an awe-inspiring experience, characteristically speaks up suggesting that they should build three shrines, one for each of the figures before them. He wants to hang on to the experience. But such an experience is not given to be fossilised but to be used, once its inner meaning has been grasped.

TEST YOURSELF ON FACTS

1. Which disciples were with Jesus on the mount of Transfiguration?
2. Which two Old Testament figures were with Jesus?
3. What did Peter say?
4. What did the voice from the cloud say?
5. What were they discussing on their way down the mountain?
6. What did Jesus say had happened to Elijah?
7. What did Jesus say when the epileptic boy's father told him his disciples had been unable to heal him?
8. What did Jesus say when the father asked if it might be possible for Jesus to heal the boy?
9. What did the father then say?
10. What reason did he give the disciples for their failure?

So Moses and Elijah vanish, leaving Jesus supreme. The Law and the Prophets are fulfilled in the coming of Christ and Jesus and his disciples come down from the mountain — down to earth in every sense of the words. But their prayers have been answered and they are now convinced that Jesus is the Messiah, whatever might happen to him.
Notice three points in the conversation as they descend:
(a) Jesus orders the three disciples to tell no one what they have seen.
(b) The time for publicity will be after he has risen from the dead, an idea which naturally puzzles them.
(c) As the disciples now know Jesus to be the Messiah they ask when Elijah will come to prepare the way for him. They are told he has already come and been rejected. *(Who was he? If you have forgotten refer to Unit 6.2)*

2. HEALING OF THE EPILEPTIC BOY

Mark 9.14 – 29: Matt. 17.14 – 20: Luke 9.37 – 43

They come straight from the transforming experience on the mountain top to the real world of sickness and pain. A crowd has gathered and it soon becomes clear that the remaining disciples have been unable to heal an epileptic boy brought to them by his father. Jesus makes it clear that their failure is due to lack of faith (Mark 9.19) and is clearly concerned that they have been so helpless without him. The whole story centres on faith.
Notice especially three points:
(a) The father's doubt ('if it is at all possible for you . . .' v.22)
(b) Jesus' reply ('Everything is possible to one who has faith.')
(c) The father's desperate plea ('I have faith, help me where faith falls short' Mark 9.24 NEB). It is the *father*'s faith which releases the healing power for his *son*.

The need for faith is emphasised in all the healing miracles. Afterwards, in private, the disciples ask Jesus the reason for their own failure and are told 'There is no means of casting out this sort but prayer' i.e. reliance on *God* rather than *self* reliance. Whatever the mode of healing, ultimately it is a function of life itself, which comes from God.

3. SECOND PREDICTION OF THE PASSION

Mark 9.30 – 32: Matt. 17.22 – 23: Luke 9.43 – 45

As they continue on their way, Jesus resumes his attempt to teach his disciples about his approaching Passion but the disciples still do not understand.

CHECK YOUR UNDERSTANDING

1. *What does the word 'transfigured' mean?*
2. *What do Moses and Elijah represent when they appear?*
3. *In what ways is the story of the Transfiguration similar to that of the Baptism of Jesus?*
4. *What is the main point of the story of the healing of the epileptic boy?*

A student member of the International Voluntary Service helping a young handicapped boy to ride a tricycle.

WHAT DO YOU THINK?
'Faith is believing what you know to be untrue.' Is this a fair definition? Can you suggest a better one?

Journey to Jerusalem

The climax of Jesus' ministry is approaching and he goes forward along the road to Jerusalem. St Mark gives us a striking picture of Jesus leading the way, striding out purposefully ahead of his disciples, his mind set on things they cannot understand as they huddle along behind him, filled with growing alarm.

1. THIRD PREDICTION OF THE PASSION

For the last time Jesus tries to make them understand what lies ahead. Only St Luke spells out the disciples' total lack of comprehension but it is clear from the next incident recorded in all three gospels that they are still blinded by dreams of thrones and crowns and of status for themselves. There is still no real comprehension of the idea of a suffering and dying Messiah.

Make sure that you know the content and the context of the predictions of the Passion. The references are as follows:

Mark 8.31; 9.31; 10.32–34	)
Matthew 16.21; 17.22–23;	) Unit 21.3 and
20.17–19	) 22.3
Luke 9.22; 9.44; 17.25; 18.31–33	)

2. QUESTION OF JAMES AND JOHN

Mark 10.35 – 45 Matt. 20.20 – 28

In St Matthew's Gospel Mrs Zebedee, the mother of James and John, comes to Jesus to ask for special privileges for her two sons. St Mark more bluntly makes the Zebedee brothers voice their own request. They ask that they may be given places of the highest honour in the Messiah's kingdom.

Thus it is made abundantly clear how little they have understood his teaching. They are still totally self-centred, even two of that 'inner circle' who had witnessed the Transfiguration. Jesus tries to help them understand that they are mistaken in their thinking. His question 'Can you drink the cup that I drink, or be baptised with the baptism I am baptised with' is a way of asking whether they are able to face suffering similar to his own. They still do not understand and say that they can. Jesus then has to tell them that, although they will in fact follow him in suffering, he himself cannot promise them such a reward. That is in God's hands.

The request inevitably causes trouble between the disciples, and Jesus patiently tries to heal the resentment simmering among the others against James and John. He explains that it is worldly people who seek power and status. 'This, however, is not the way it is among you.' Again he stresses that true greatness lies in service, 'For even the Son of Man did not come to be served; he came to serve and to give his life to redeem many people.' (v.45 GNB) The word 'redeem' = 'buy back, pay the purchase price for a slave.' The use of the word suggests that Jesus sees himself as about to do something for many people which they cannot do for themselves — purchase their freedom (*from what?*)

3. HEALING OF BARTIMAEUS

Mark 10.46 – 52: Matt. 20.29 – 34: Luke 18.35 – 43

Learn accurately the details of this story in whichever gospel forms part of your syllabus and be careful not to confuse it with the healing of the blind man of Bethsaida. Notice that St Matthew tells us there were two blind men whereas St Mark and St Luke speak only of one. It is St. Mark who tells us the man's name was Bartimaeus (Bar = 'son of').

Notice the following points:

(a) The blind man addresses Jesus as 'Son of David', one of the titles of the Messiah. He has 'seen' who Jesus really is, despite his physical blindness and in marked contrast to the 'blindness' of most people.

(b) Jesus no longer tries to silence public recognition of himself as Messiah. He is on his way to Jerusalem for the last time. Premature recognition is no longer a threat.

(c) The beggar *persists* despite all discouragement. The crowd do not want Jesus pestered by a

TEST YOURSELF ON FACTS

1. What request did the Zebedee brothers (or their mother) make to Jesus?
2. What did he reply?
3. What did Jesus say to the rest of the disciples who were angry with James and John?
4. What was the name of the blind man in Jericho?
5. What did he shout as Jesus passed by?
6. What did Jesus then say?
7. What did Jesus say had healed him?
8. Who did Jesus send to fetch the donkey as he approached Jerusalem?
9. What were the disciples to say when challenged?
10. What is the meaning of Hosanna?

beggar but he refuses to be silenced. It is, in a literal sense, his chance of a lifetime to be healed. He has faith in Jesus' power to cure him but, if he allows Jesus to pass by without noticing his helpless plight, he will be condemned to lifelong blindness.

(d) There is an interesting contrast between St Mark and St Luke's account in which, unexpectedly, Mark gives us the more vivid impression of the beggar's personality. St Luke, doubtless thinking of blind people of his acquaintance, tells us that Jesus ordered the blind man *to be brought to him,* whereas St Mark tells us he *'threw off his cloak, jumped up, and came to Jesus'* — a much more determinedly independent action and one more in keeping with the sturdy persistence of Bartimaeus in his search for healing.

4. TRIUMPHAL ENTRY INTO JERUSALEM

Mark 11.1 – 11: Matt. 21.1 – 11: Luke 19.28 – 40

The climax of Jesus' ministry is approaching when he will show himself as Messiah and so give people the opportunity to accept him as such. It is a situation fraught with danger for him personally but he is quite sure that God intends him to take this step — hence that determined setting of his face towards Jerusalem.

What happens from now onwards needs to be seen against a background of Messianic prophecy. Jerusalem is not just the political capital of Israel; it is the holy city where God resides among his people as he had 'tabernacled' among them in the wilderness in the time of Moses. The Messiah, as king of the Jews, was expected to arrive in his capital city riding on a donkey from the Mount of Olives.

There is symbolism even in his mode of transport. The prophets rode donkeys, showing that they came in peace. A king arriving on a horse would foreshadow his going to war. What better way of alerting the Jews to Jesus' identity than fulfilling the prophecies?

So Jesus makes preparations in advance to fulfil the prophecy of Zechariah. Had Jesus not made these plans in advance it is difficult to account for the instruction he gives to his disciples in Mark 11.1 – 3 and equally to account for the owner's acquiescence in their removing his donkey — unless you are prepared to believe that Jesus was possessed of magical powers and knew that there was a donkey waiting, with an easy-going owner prepared to see two strangers walk off with it. Assuming Jesus had made arrangements in advance, 'The Lord has need of it' then becomes a password by which the authorised disciples could be identified. We shall see other evidence of forward planning as the week advances.

● ***PROPHECY:*** Zechariah 9.9

'Rejoice greatly, O daughter of Zion; shout, O daughter of Jerusalem: behold, thy King cometh unto thee: he is just, and having salvation; lowly, and riding upon an ass, and upon a colt the foal of an ass.' (AV)

This prophecy probably accounts for St Matthew's telling us there were both an ass and *a colt. Remember how often he refers to the Old Testament (Unit 1.2(c)(iii)). Writing with the prophecy in mind, he failed to recognise that the last phrase is poetic repetition — a technique frequently used in Hebrew poetry and known as 'parallelism' — and assumed there must have been two animals since Zechariah had said there would be when he wrote 500 years earlier.*

PALM SUNDAY

Christians recall this event on the Sunday before Easter. The Synoptic Gospels only refer to 'leafy branches'. It is St John's Gospel which tells us they were 'palm branches' (John 12.13), from which the day gets its name.

Palm crosses are distributed to those taking part who then walk in procession to the church (on this occasion symbolising the holy city where God dwells) singing such well-known hymns as 'Ride on, ride on in majesty' and 'All glory, laud and honour'. In recent years some parishes have imported a donkey to join in the procession. The Church is, in fact, acting out the events of Christ's arrival in Jerusalem.

The donkey is brought and Jesus mounts it. It would have been in accordance with usual practice that an animal intended for religious use should not have previously been used for ordinary purposes. But try mounting an unbroken donkey yourself and see what happens to you! We can only assume that the animal instinctively recognised both the authority and the peacefulness of Jesus and responded.

The procession sets off and the people spread their cloaks on the road in front of Jesus (something which has been done as a sign of respect to great people throughout history.)

Was this great crowd welcoming Jesus and acknowledging him as Messiah? 'Hosanna' is a Hebrew word meaning 'Save now' and could be taken as a recognition of Jesus as the Messiah. On the other hand, by the end of the week, the crowds were shouting 'Crucify him' so their recognition could not have been very deep seated. It seems more probable that the little crowd of Galilean pilgrims surrounding Jesus took up the cry. They had seen and heard more of him than the people of Jerusalem and so perhaps were more ready to make the leap of faith. The city people did not join in (Matt. 21.10). They said 'Who is this?' and were told 'This is our prophet from Galilee.' The shouting seems to have been part of the pilgrimage procession. Normally psalms would have been recited on the journey (Nos. 120–134) and the priests would welcome pilgrims coming to the Feast in the words of Psalm 118.26, 'Blessed be he that cometh in the name of the Lord' (AV), so it seems that the Hosannas punctuated the normal singing of psalms on the journey.

Thus Jesus is claiming to be the Messiah by entering Jerusalem in this way. There is still a chance that he may carry the crowds with him and introduce the Messianic Age, though he himself had already rejected the way of a kingly Messiah (Luke 4.1–13: Unit 7.2(b)). On the other hand, readers of the gospels know that this is the beginning of Holy Week, the week in which, day by day, Christians recall the events of the Passion (= suffering) of Christ.

CHECK YOUR UNDERSTANDING

1. *What do you understand by the request of James and John 'to sit one at your right hand and one at your left'?*
2. *What did Jesus mean by 'drinking the cup' and 'baptism' on this occasion?*
3. *In what way does Jesus' idea of greatness differ from that of the disciples?*
4. *What is significant about Bartimaeus addressing Jesus as 'Son of David'?*
5. *What is symbolic in Jesus' mode of arrival in Jerusalem?*
6. *What evidence is there in this story that Jesus had made plans in advance? Give reasons for your answer.*
7. *Why did people spread their cloaks on the road in front of Jesus?*
8. *In what way did Jesus' understanding of Messiahship differ from that of the crowds?*

WHAT DO YOU THINK?

1. Jesus corrects his disciples' ideas of greatness. How would you (a) define greatness (b) recognise a great person? Choose a living person whom you regard as great, research his/her life and tell the class about him/her.
2. Is anything to be gained by celebrating events year by year? Consider, for example, trooping the colour to celebrate the Queen's birthday. What effect do you think the event has on participants? Is the effect on onlookers different? Is the celebration worth the trouble?

The Temple

So the Messiah comes to the Temple and, if we are to understand what happens next, we need to know something about what the Temple meant to the Jews and how it functioned.

1. THE TEMPLE

The Temple built by Herod the Great (the one Jesus would have known) was the third Temple to be built on the site. Traditionally it is the spot where Abraham prepared to sacrifice Isaac (Gen.22) and inside the Dome of the Rock (the mosque which now occupies the site) the rock where this is said to have happened is exposed, reminding us that this is a most holy place for Muslims as well as for Jews and Christians.

King Solomon built the first Temple during the tenth century BC and its building is described in detail in 1 Kings 5–8. No expense was spared. Only the finest materials were used and they were overlaid with gold. The building was small, comparable in size with a small chapel rather than a great cathedral, and was designed as a 'home' for God among his people rather than as a place for large congregations to meet for worship. This first Temple was destroyed in 597 BC by Nebuchadnezzar, King of Babylon (Jer. 52.13) and a second Temple was built during the reign of Zerubbabel around the year 516 BC. This second Temple in turn was looted and destroyed until finally Herod the Great cleared the site and started building again about twenty years before the birth of Jesus. This third Temple too was doomed, being destroyed by the Romans in AD 70 but, at the time of Jesus, it would have been a magnificent sight

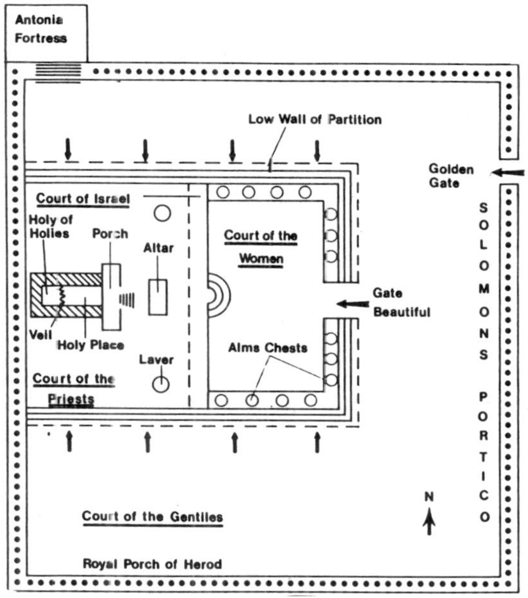

Plan of Herod's Temple.

built of snow white marble encrusted with gold. It was not finished until about five years before its destruction so building work would still have been in progress when Jesus arrived.

There were four courtyards built on rising ground. The outer one and the lowest was the **Court of the Gentiles**. It was open to anybody although a large red-painted sign (found by archeologists in 1935) prohibited non-Jews from going beyond a certain point on pain of death.

The next courtyard, the **Court of the Women**, was open to Jews of either sex provided they were physically sound. Beyond that was the **Court of Israel**, open to Jewish males over the age of twelve and beyond that came the **Court of the Priests**. Here stood the altar before the **Holy Place** which itself contained the altar of incense and the seven-branched candelabra. It would have been here that Zechariah had his vision when he was told that his wife would have a child. Separated from the Holy Place only by a curtain was the innermost sanctuary, the Holy of Holies which was kept in darkness and into which only the High Priest might go and that on only one day in the year, the Day of Atonement. The most striking thing about the Holy of Holies was that it contained no statue as similar temples in honour of pagan gods invariably did, and the structure of the whole Temple emphasised that God could only be approached through becoming a Jew. Gentiles might come to worship but were kept at a distance from the Holy of Holies. Here priests offered up prescribed sacrifices not only for the personal milestones of life, such as the birth of a child or some other occasion for thankfulness, but also at the great festivals of the

TEST YOURSELF ON FACTS

1. Who built the first Temple?
2. Who built the Temple Jesus would have known?
3. What building occupies the site today?
4. What was the purpose of the Court of the Gentiles?
5. Who could use the Court of the Women?
6. What would one have found in (a) the Holy Place (b) the Holy of Holies?
7. Why were there moneychangers in the Temple?
8. What had the prophet Malachi predicted of the Messiah?
9. What had Isaiah written about God's intention for his house?

Jewish calendar, the greatest of which was Passover. The animals provided for these sacrifices had to be unblemished and, although there was nothing to stop an individual taking along his own animal for the sacrifice, it was usually more convenient to buy the animal in the Temple where its suitability was guaranteed. When it came to paying for the animal — or, for that matter, paying the Temple tax which was levied on all Jews — it was necessary to change currency. The ordinary everyday coins bore the head of Caesar who was worshipped by the occupying Roman forces as a god. Consequently the Jews would not allow the image of a pagan 'god' inside the Temple and special Temple coins were minted known as Holy Shekels. Visitors to the Temple had first of all to change their money. All this commercial activity went on in the Court of the Gentiles and was under the control of the Temple authorities. It was not a case of a quick-witted merchant finding a good pitch near the Temple until he was moved on by the police; the whole system was organised by the religious authorities themselves and went on inside the Temple — in the Court of Gentiles — and had become an accepted part of Temple life.

2. OVERTHROWING OF THE MONEY CHANGERS

Mark 11.15 – 17: Matt. 21.12 – 17: Luke 19.45 – 48

Against the background of the above knowledge of what the Temple meant in Jewish life the next action of Jesus is seen in a new light.

Notice the following points:

(a) Jesus is not challenging something *illegal*, as a good man might question whether goods on sale in a shady street market had 'dropped off the back of a lorry'. In attacking a long-established practice in the Temple, he is challenging the very religious authorities who were responsible for upholding standards of right in the nation.

(b) The prophet Malachi had spoken of the Messiah coming to the Temple to cleanse it and that is what Jesus does, thus offering those with 'eyes to see' the opportunity of acknowledging him as Messiah.

> ● ***PROPHECY*** Malachi 3.1 – 3
>
> *'. . . and the Lord, whom ye seek, shall suddenly come to his temple, even the messenger of the covenant, whom ye delight in: behold, he shall come, saith the Lord of hosts. But who may abide the day of his coming? and who shall stand when he appeareth? for he is like a refiner's fire, and like fullers' soap: And he shall sit as a refiner and purifier of silver: and he shall purify the sons of Levi, and purge them as gold and silver, that they may offer unto the Lord an offering in righteousness.' (AV)*

CHECK YOUR UNDERSTANDING

1. *In what way did the structure of the Temple emphasise that the way to approach God was through becoming a Jew?*
2. *Why was it customary to buy sacrificial animals in the Temple itself?*
3. *Why was it necessary to change Roman coins into Holy shekels?*
4. *In what way was Jesus' action in the Temple Messianic?*
5. *What was his purpose in cleansing the Temple?*

(c) Thus far is common to all the gospels but St Mark makes explicit one extra point. The market place occupied the Court of the Gentiles. Thus Jewish worship was undisturbed by animal noises and the voices of money changers, but Gentiles coming to the Temple to worship had nowhere quiet for prayer. All three writers record Jesus' saying, in the words of Isaiah (56.7) 'mine house shall be called an house of prayer', but only St Mark gives us the last three words, '*for all people*', i.e. Jesus is restoring to Gentiles their place in God's house.
The rest of what Jesus says, 'but you have made it a den of robbers' (RSV) is a quotation from Jeremiah 7.11.

(d) The episode ends with the ominous threat 'they began looking for some way to kill Jesus.' (Mark 11.18 GNB)

WHAT DO YOU THINK?

1. Is it wrong to spend large sums of money on beautifying cathedrals and churches when there are millions in the world dying of starvation?
2. A few years ago the authorities at Rochester cathedral decided to sell some church treasures to help finance the building of a visitors' centre. This communion silver had been given to the cathedral hundreds of years ago and there was much criticism of the sale. What do you think?

Test Questions

Because the Temple authorities cannot risk arresting someone as popular as Jesus for fear of a riot, they try tactics to discredit him instead. One by one they send him questioners, each with a two-edged problem so that, whichever answer Jesus gives, he is bound to make himself unpopular with one or other of the groups who might otherwise be interested in his teaching. In this way they hope the number of his supporters will dwindle and he himself become isolated and so fall into their power.
First of all remind yourselves of the nature of these different bodies — the scribes (Unit 10.1), the Pharisees (Unit 10.2) Herodians (Unit 10.5), priests and Levites (Unit 14.4). Another group, not yet described, were the Sadducees.

● *SADDUCEES*

Sadducees were an aristocratic party found mainly in Jerusalem and the High Priests were chosen from their ranks. They were an extremely conservative group, small in number (only a few hundred) but politically powerful. They accepted the authority of the Torah but would have nothing to do with the Tradition of the Elders. They therefore rejected such 'modern' beliefs as angels and life after death and they strenuously resisted religious change. Falling foul of them was dangerous because of their political influence.

In each of these four test questions you need to learn:
(a) The question
(b) The questioners and why the question is appropriate to their particular group.
(c) The answer.

BE SURE TO READ THE TEXT CAREFULLY IN EACH CASE.

1. 'BY WHAT AUTHORITY . . .?'

Mark 11.27 – 33: Matt. 21.23 – 27: Luke 20.1 – 8

(a) **THE QUESTION**

This is in two parts:
(i) By what authority do you do these things?
(ii) Who gave you this authority?

The snag in this question is that religious authority for the Jews was vested in the very people who were asking the question i.e. members of the Sanhedrin.

● *SANHEDRIN*

The Sanhedrin was a Council in Jerusalem made up of seventy-one members under the chairmanship of the High Priest. It had supreme authority among the Jews in all matters of religion and justice and was controlled by Sadducees. It was recognised by the Romans as the representative Council of the Jews and, because its members were concerned to maintain their authority, they were concerned to maintain reasonable relations with the Romans.

(b) **THE QUESTIONERS**

Chief priests, teachers of the law and elders made up the Sanhedrin. As the Sanhedrin was the supreme Jewish authority, it is appropriate for them to question Jesus about the source of his authority. The catch lies in the fact that, if Jesus replies that his authority comes from God, he lays himself open to a charge of blasphemy. He cannot say he has been authorised to teach by the Sanhedrin because he hasn't and they know it.

(c) **THE ANSWER**

As on many other occasions, Jesus replies by asking another question — Where did John the Baptist's authority come from? Jesus has turned the tables on them! If they say John's authority came from God, Jesus' next question will obviously be, 'Then why didn't you pillars of the religious establishment do as he said?' If, on the other hand, they say that John's authority was merely human, they will be in trouble with ordinary people who regarded John as a very great prophet.
Round One to Jesus!

2. PAYMENT OF TAXES TO CAESAR

Mark 12.13 – 17: Matt. 22.15 – 22: Luke 20.20 – 26

(a) **THE QUESTION**

This question is designed to cause Jesus maximum embarrassment. If he replies 'No, it is contrary to Jewish law to pay taxes to a pagan

Roman Emperor,' the authorities can hand him over to the Romans who would sentence him to death as an agitator. If, on the other hand, he agrees to the payment of taxes, he would lose the support of the Jewish crowds.

(b) **THE QUESTIONERS**

Pharisees and Herodians join forces to entrap Jesus this time (refer to Mark 3.6). The Pharisees made no fuss about payment of taxes. They felt the Romans were fair, allowing reasonable freedom of worship and providing fairly even-handed justice in a country where there were endless local squabbles.

(c) **THE ANSWER**

Jesus asks his questioners to produce a coin — a skilful move. The Romans, in fact, went to the lengths of producing a coin without Caesar's head on it for circulation in Palestine, in deference to the strong religious feeling of the Jews, although many ordinary Roman coins were also in circulation. Yet these Pharisees and Herodians who profess to have such strong views on the subject have no difficulty in producing one of the controversial coins. Point One to Jesus.

CHECK YOUR UNDERSTANDING

1. *Where was the trap in the question asked by members of the Sanhedrin?*
2. *Why were they unable to reply to Jesus' counter-question?*
3. *Where was the trap in the question about payment of taxes to Caesar?*
4. *Explain Jesus' pronouncement at the end of this story.*
5. *To what custom was the Sadducee referring in his story about the woman who married seven brothers in turn?*
6. *Why does Jesus refer to the story of Moses at the burning bush?*
7. *Why is the interpretation of the Parable of the Wicked Tenants usually taken to be the work of the early Church?*
8. *List the similarities between this parable and the Song of the Vineyard in Isaiah 5.1 – 7.*
9. *In what way can Jesus be regarded as the cornerstone?*
10. *What was the significance of the woman anointing Jesus?*

He then says in effect that Caesar controls all the money bearing his head so, in paying taxes, they are only giving him what he already possesses. 'But,' adds Jesus, 'don't forget your obligation to God too.'

The saying is another famous yardstick for all time. Christians have frequently had to live under pagan authority (as in Russia today). Jesus says there is no disloyalty to God in obeying a pagan government, *provided it does not interfere with the Christian's duty to God*.

ARE YOU STILL READING
THE TEXT EACH TIME?

---

3. QUESTION ABOUT RESURRECTION

Mark 12.18 – 27: Matt. 22.23 – 33: Luke 20.27 – 40

We have already seen (Unit 3.1) that Jews regarded childlessness as a great affliction and it was their custom (Deut. 25.5), when a man died without having had children, for his next of kin to marry the widow and their children would count as those of the dead man.

(a) **THE QUESTION**

Here is a question about a woman who married seven husbands in turn in order to produce an heir. Surely a case of the kiss of death! At the end of it all she is still childless and then dies herself. At the resurrection, whose wife will she be?

(b) **THE QUESTIONER**

This time the questioner is a Sadducee and, as Sadducees do not believe in resurrection, since it is not mentioned in the Torah, it is clear he had no interest in a possible answer and is just out to trap Jesus.

(c) **THE ANSWER**

Jesus' answer falls into two parts:

(i) The question is nonsense since one cannot apply the standards of this life to life in a different dimension where marriage as an institution does not exist.

(ii) Jesus nevertheless supports belief in life after death. He quotes the incident when God calls Moses at the burning bush (Exod.3.6) and points out that God says 'I AM the God of Abraham, Isaac and Jacob', not 'I WAS their God'. Therefore Abraham, Isaac and Jacob must still be alive somewhere.

4. THE CHIEF COMMANDMENT

Mark 12.28 – 34: Matt. 22.34 – 40: Luke 10.25 – 28

Notice that, in St Luke's Gospel, this is the question which leads Jesus to tell the parable of the Good Samaritan (Unit 14.4).

(a) **THE QUESTION**

The question of which commandment is the most important of all was reasonable enough when it is remembered that the Tradition of the Elders counted 613 of them! There are two ways of looking at this incident:

(i) In the context of the battle of wits in which Jesus is engaged, it is perhaps reasonable to see it as another challenge to Jesus. Discussion of the relative importance of the commandments was common among the rabbis and the scribe may have anticipated being able to tie Jesus in knots.

(ii) On the other hand, if a man were being charged with heresy (= untrue belief) he could be challenged to quote the great commandment. If he quoted correctly, he was safe. It is possible that this particular scribe was offering Jesus just such a lifeline, a fact which Jesus acknowledges when he says. 'You are not far from the kingdom of God.' (Mark verse 34).

(b) **THE QUESTIONER**

For 'scribes' see Unit 10.1.

(c) **THE ANSWER**

Jesus brings together two quotations from the Old Testament (Deut. 6.4 and Lev. 19.18) which any rabbi would have used to summarise the law. All the rest of the teaching of the Law and the Prophets depends on these twin duties of love of God and love of neighbour. Religious life is the working out of a balance between them.

Jesus has won the arguments. The evangelists all tell us 'After this nobody dared to ask Jesus any more questions.'

5. PARABLE OF THE WICKED TENANTS

Mark 12.1 – 12: Matt. 21.33 – 46: Luke 20.9 – 19

Jesus tells this parable during the time of his deepening quarrel with the religious authorities. Since the interpretation is usually allegorised (See Unit 14.1(d)) we are probably correct in assuming that it owed its present form to the Early Church. In order to understand it, you need to be familiar with an Old Testament parable in Isaiah 5.1 – 7. In this story God had chosen Israel as his own vine. He had planted it and lovingly cared for it but, when the time came to harvest the fruit (*what does this represent*?) every grape was sour.

From this it became clear that the vineyard in Jesus' story stands for Israel and the householder represents God. The tenants are the Jewish people, the servants are the prophets and the only Son, of course, is Jesus himself. The whole story is about God's dealings with his people, ending with the letting of the vineyard to 'other tenants' i.e. the new people of God, the Church. The scripture quoted by Jesus in verse 10 is Psalm 118.22 which refers to a tradition that, when Solomon's Temple was being built, a stone was found on the site which seemed to have no obvious purpose and so it was thrown away. Later, the cornerstone which binds together two walls was missing and the rejected stone was found to be the one for which everyone was searching. It is not difficult to see how early Christians applied this tradition to the person of Jesus himself.

6. QUESTION ABOUT THE MESSIAH

Mark 12.35 – 37: Matt. 22.41 – 46: Luke 20.41 – 44

Jesus himself now takes up the questioning and asks why his hearers believe that the Messiah must be descended from King David. He quotes from Psalm 110.1 (at the time the psalms were believed to have been written by King David) in which the poet refers to the Messiah as 'My Lord.' One does not usually address one's children, or many-times-great-grandchildren as 'My Lord'. Therefore the idea that the Messiah must be descended from King David is denied in scripture itself.

TEST YOURSELF ON FACTS

1. What question was asked by chief priests, the teachers of the Law and the elders?
2. How did Jesus reply to them?
3. Who asked the question about paying taxes to Caesar?
4. What pronouncement did Jesus make at the end of this story?
5. Who asked about resurrection?
6. What does Jesus say about resurrection?
7. How does Jesus summarise the commandments?
8. In the parable of the wicked tenants, what do the following represent (a) the vineyard, (b) the householder (c) the servants (d) the only son (e) 'other tenants'?
9. What comment does Jesus make on the Messiah being descended from David?
10. What did Jesus say about the woman who anointed him?

7. ANOINTING AT BETHANY

Mark 14.3 – 9: Matt. 26.6 – 13

One other story intervenes before the drama of the betrayal, arrest, trials and crucifixion of Jesus begins.

Jesus is staying at Bethany, in the house of Simon the leper. This was almost certainly the home of Martha, Mary and their brother Lazarus (= 'leper') where Jesus was always made welcome. A woman comes with a beautiful jar of expensive perfume which she breaks and pours over Jesus' head. There are a number of points to notice:

(a) The word 'Messiah' = 'anointed one.' Possibly this was a recognition by the woman that Jesus was the Messiah. Certainly anointing of this kind was reserved for very important people indeed.

(b) The woman *broke* the flask. Such flasks of perfume were very valuable. A woman might be given one on her marriage to last a lifetime. She would not normally break such a beautiful object. Yet there is evidence that, when a corpse was anointed for burial, the flask *was* broken. So there is symbolism in this incident, even if to the woman herself it was unintentional. Christians reading the gospel would know that there had been no time to pepare Jesus' body for burial on Good Friday yet these last rites had been performed, albeit unwittingly, in advance.

(c) Those at the meal are angry with the woman for her apparently wanton waste, but Jesus will not allow a loving action to be criticised. So we see not only the loving regard which Jesus evokes in ordinary people but also his gentle understanding of them.

(d) The original story may well have ended with the pronouncement of Jesus in verse 7, 'You will always have the poor with you.' There will be many other opportunities to serve those in need but not many more to honour him. Increasingly Jesus seems to be aware that time is running out.

A glass flask of the Roman period found in Jerusalem.

WHAT DO YOU THINK?

1. Mahatma Gandhi said that when authority is misused e.g. when laws are passed which are morally wrong, the individual has a duty to break that law *and suffer the consequences*. In that way moral pressure is brought to bear to change the law. Investigate examples of such action in his own life.
2. In our own times people sometimes withold payment of tax on the grounds of disapproving of the way in which the government spends the money (e.g. on missiles). Does the teaching of Jesus give encouragement to their action? Give reasons for your answer.

The Betrayal and the Last Supper

Be sure to read the text carefully before you turn to the notes.

1. THE BETRAYAL

Mark 14.10 – 11: Matt. 26.14 – 16: Luke 22.3 – 6

(a) WHY DID JUDAS ISCARIOT BETRAY JESUS?

The reason is not clear from the gospel narrative. Here are some suggestions for you to consider:

(i) *For money.* St Matthew tells us Judas was paid thirty pieces of silver — not a vast sum of money. Would you betray your friend to a horrifying death for money? There is no reason to doubt that Judas was paid for his information, but is it likely that money was his *motive*?

(ii) *Fear.* It must have been increasingly clear that Jesus was heading for very serious trouble and that his disciples would then be in great danger too. By betraying Jesus, Judas may have hoped to save his own skin.

(iii) *Disappointment.* Jesus was not behaving as Judas believed the Messiah should. Some people think Judas believed that, if he put Jesus into a tight corner, he would force him to show his power. It never crossed his mind, despite all the teaching about a suffering Messiah, that Jesus would stick to the path he had chosen. When his plan did not work Judas was filled with remorse.

(iv) *Wickedness.* St Luke tells us 'Satan entered Judas' — a sudden change of character? Such things do not happen like a bolt from the blue but grow out of existing flaws of personality. Judas was probably the cleverest of the disciples — he was treasurer of the little band. Was he growing impatient with a situation he felt he could manage better himself?

(b) WHAT DID JUDAS BETRAY?

There is no mention of evidence from Judas in the accounts of the trials of Jesus. It seems that his contribution to the passion narrative lies in leading the police to the place where he knew Jesus would be alone with his disciples. The Sanhedrin could not risk the open daylight arrest of such a popular figure when Jerusalem was crowded with pilgrims. Seizing him quietly at night avoided the risk of a riot.

2. PREPARATION FOR THE LAST SUPPER

Mark 14.12 – 16: Matt. 26.17 – 19: Luke 22.7 – 13

In the same way that Jesus had made advance preparation for his entry into Jerusalem (Unit 23.4) he seems also to have made advance plans for a last secret meal with his disciples. It was a dangerous operation for him personally. He knew that the authorities would seize the first opportunity to arrest him. For safety's sake, he was staying outside the city but had made arrangements to meet in the upper room of the house of a friend (probably Mark's mother). A group of twelve men would be conspicuous in the narrow streets of Jerusalem so he sent two in advance to make the preparations (Luke tells us they were Peter and John) and the rest were to follow later, probably in twos and threes.

A secret signal had been prepared so that the advance party could recognise the guide who would lead them to their rendezvous. To save having to ask the way and so risk the discovery of their secret destination, they were to look out for a man carrying a water pot — a bizarre and extremely unusual sight in a society where only women carried water pots. This guide would lead them to the correct house.

TEST YOURSELF ON FACTS

1. Who betrayed Jesus?
2. What was he paid for his information?
3. Who went ahead to prepare the passover meal?
4. How were they to know where to go?
5. What were they to say to the owner of the house?
6. What did Jesus do/say when he took a piece of bread?
7. What did Jesus do/say when he took a cup of wine?
8. What did they do before they left the table?
9. What Jewish celebration is associated with the last supper?
10. Which Christian act of worship commemorates it?

3. THE LAST SUPPER

Mark 14.17 – 26: Matt. 26.20 – 30: Luke 22.14 – 38

(a) CONNECTION WITH PASSOVER

Without going into detail, you need to be aware that there is a difference between the Synoptic Gospels and the Fourth Gospel over the question of whether or not the Last Supper was a Passover meal. According to the Synoptic Gospels it was, but the Fourth Gospel tells us that Jesus died on the Day of Preparation, when the passover lambs were being killed. The significant symbolism of this fact will become apparent shortly. Which version was correct? On the whole it seems more probable that St John is correct because, if the Last Supper had been a Passover meal, it would mean that the arrest, trial and crucifixion had taken place at the height of the greatest Jewish festival. It seems very unlikely that the Jews would have allowed Passover to have been profaned in this way.

There are two possible explanations for the Synoptic Gospels describing the Last Supper as a Passover meal:

(i) Jesus, knowing he was going to be arrested very soon and wanting to leave his disciples with some indelible teaching linked to the great festival, brought the meal forward by twenty-four hours. If you were going to be flying to Australia on Christmas Day, your family might well celebrate Christmas a day early so that you could be with them.

(ii) An alternative theory is that the meal may have been a Passover kiddush — a meal shared by strict Jews in preparation for Passover.

(b) ANNOUNCEMENT OF THE TRAITOR

Remember that a shared meal was a sign of close fellowship so that Jesus' saying that there was a traitor in their midst naturally upset the disciples. Mark only tells us that the traitor was present. Matthew tells us that Jesus singled him out. The dish into which he was dipping his bread with Jesus was possibly that which contained the charoseth paste.

> **OLD TESTAMENT IDEA OF SACRIFICE**
> **A sacrifice was regarded as a bridge between God and man. It was believed that the life of the animal was present in its blood. When the animal was killed, that life was released. When an agreement was made between men, it was customary to offer a sacrifice and to sprinkle some of the blood of the animal onto both parties; in this way they were bound together through the life of the sacrificial victim.**
> **The disciples would have had this belief in mind as Jesus went through the solemn actions at the Last Supper.**

> ● ***PASSOVER***
> *The origin of Passover can be found in Exodus 12 where we are told how God led the Israelites out of slavery in Egypt towards freedom and the promised land. He made a covenant with them in which they became his own people. Each year since then, that great occasion has been recalled by Jews everywhere. It is not a matter of just remembering something which happened long, long ago but rather of entering imaginatively into the events so that each individual Jew makes them his own. It is as though each one were experiencing God's deliverance from slavery as he or she recalls the greatest moment of their history. Passover is a family gathering. Much careful preparation is made and at the passover meal itself a special order of service is used (known as the Haggadah). The youngest child present asks questions ('Why is this night different from all other nights?') and, in answering the questions the father of the family retells the story of their deliverance.*
> *Special foods are eaten to remind them of what happened — roast lamb, bitter herbs, salt water, unleavened bread, a special sweet paste known as charoseth and four cups of wine are drunk. The meal ends with the singing of special songs and the asking of a blessing.*
> *In the days of Jesus the food was set out on a low table, the guests reclining around it on their left elbows with their feet stretched out behind them. No knives and forks were used, the guests eating with the fingers of their right hands. As you study the gospel accounts of the Last Supper, bear in mind these different elements of the Passover meal.*

Mark 14.21 is important. Although the evangelists make it clear that the death of Jesus was part of God's plan for the salvation of the world, those who brought it about cannot be excused from responsibility for their action.

(c) THE MEAL

What happened next needs to be seen in relation to:

(i) Passover
(ii) Holy Communion (the Eucharist/Mass/ Lord's Supper).

(i) *Passover*

Jesus used the ordinary actions of a Jewish father at a Passover meal. He *took* the unleavened bread, said a prayer of *thanks*, *broke* it and *gave* it to those sitting at table with him. *Recall the actions of Jesus in the feeding miracles* (Unit 12.3(c)).

A priest consecrating the bread and wine at Holy Communion.

The words he spoke, however, would have been electrifying — 'Take; this is my body.' (v 22 RSV). These words would have suggested to the disciples that they were being invited to share in the body of a sacrificial victim.

Similarly in the words over the cup of wine — one of the four cups drunk at Passover — Jesus described the wine as 'my blood of the covenant' thus again suggesting that he himself was to be the sacrifice.

So, in the same way that Passover celebrated the action of God in saving the Israelites from slavery and making them his own chosen people, the Last Supper created a new people of God and a new covenant (= agreement) sealed in the blood of Jesus.

(ii) *Holy Communion/the Eucharist/Mass/Lord's Supper.*

The earliest account of this meal occurs, not in the gospels, but in St Paul's first letter to the Corinthians (11.23–25). Here six words are included which the gospel writers do not record — 'Do this in memory of me.' Possibly by the time the gospels were written a celebration of this meal had become such an important part of Christian life that it was thought unnecessary to include these words of command. Why *do* Christians 'do this'? In obedience to Christ. Although there are very many different shades of understanding of its meaning in the different Christian denominations, all would agree that Holy Communion, by whatever name, is the central act of Christian worship. For some it is so important that it is celebrated daily; for others it is so important that it is celebrated more rarely to ensure that it is never taken for granted.

The act is a sacrament — an outward sign (bread and wine) of an inward gift of God. Some Christians think of this service as a way of remembering what Jesus did for them; others believe that Christ himself comes to them in a very special way when they 'eat Christ's body and drink his blood'. In the Fourth Gospel Jesus is recorded as saying, 'Whoever eats my flesh and drinks my blood lives in me, and I live in him' (John 6.56). So, when the bread and the wine are received in faith, they unite believers with Christ and with each other. Christians reading the story of the Last Supper have in mind not only what happened that night but also see the occasion in the light of the death and resurrection which were to follow so soon after it.

CHECK YOUR UNDERSTANDING

1. *Suggest three possible reasons for the traitor's betraying Jesus.*
2. *What indication is there that Jesus had made secret preparations in advance for the Last Supper?*
3. *What indications are there that the Last Supper may have been a passover meal?*
4. *How was the meal set out and eaten?*
5. *On what other occasion earlier in his ministry did Jesus perform the same actions with bread?*
6. *What is the significance of calling the wine 'my blood of the covenant'?*
7. *What is a sacrament?*
8. *Why is this occasion so important for Christians?*

• *VARIATIONS IN ST LUKE'S GOSPEL*

For those studying the Passion narrative in St Luke's Gospel, the following list of variations from St Mark will be useful:

(i) The cup is taken before the bread

(ii) There is an argument among the disciples about which of them is the greatest, (Luke 22.24–30). Jesus' reply is similar to his response to the question of James and John in Mark 10.35–45 (Unit 23.2).

(iii) Sifting of Simon
Jesus knows that someone of Simon's temperament will be likely to fail in the kind of cold-blooded crisis which lies ahead but notice that he says, 'When you turn back to me, you must strengthen your brothers.' He shows a faith in him which is to be justified after the resurrection. The prediction of Peter's denials comes later in Mark and Matthew and is considered at the beginning of Unit 27.

(iv) Jesus reminds the disciples of the early days in Galilee when he had ordered them to 'travel light'. Now they must be ready to find everyone against them. The disciples show they are ready with swords. Jesus' reply, 'That is enough,' is taken literally by some commentators but others suggest it is a despairing dismissal of the whole subject. They still do not understand.

INVESTIGATION

Try to visit Churches of at least two different denominations when they are celebrating this particular service. Alternatively your teacher may invite ministers from different denominations to come and explain what they do and why. An interesting comparison would be between a Roman Catholic or an Anglican on one side (what difference do you see between their practices?) and a Baptist or the United Reformed Church on the other. You might also invite a Quaker to explain their attitude to it.

Gethsemane: Trial before the High Priest. Peter's Denials

1. PREDICTION OF PETER'S DENIALS

Mark 14.27 – 31: Matt. 26.31 – 35: Luke 22.31 – 34

As they leave the Upper Room and walk through the city gate and down the steep slope to the river Kidron and across to the Mount of Olives, Jesus tells the disciples that they will all leave him and run away. In the words of Zechariah 13.7 he uses the imagery of the killing of the shepherd and the scattering of his sheep. In other words, Old Testament prophecy is about to be fulfilled. Yet there is light at the end of the tunnel — 'But after I am raised to life, I will go to Galilee ahead of you.' (GNB) What could the disciples have made of such a statement?

Once again it is Peter who will not hear of Jesus' death. (Remember his reaction to the first prediction of the Passion in Matt. 16.22: Unit 21.3). Jesus assures him that before the cock crows *twice*, Peter will have denied him *three* times.

Cockcrow was the name given to the bugle call which signalled the change of guard for the Romans in the small hours of the morning (Lat. *gallicinium*). It seems people were not allowed to keep cocks in Jerusalem in the days of Christ. Nevertheless the cock soon became a symbol of watchfulness in the early Church and even today many churches are adorned with weathercocks.

2. GETHSEMANE

Mark 14.32 – 42: Matt. 26.36 – 46: Luke 22.39 – 46

First, remind yourself of the Temptations in the wilderness (Unit 7.2) Jesus had made his decision about his ministry at that time but, now the climax has been reached, the temptation to avoid suffering is redoubled.

Learn what happened accurately i.e.

(a) Jesus leaves eight of the disciples on the edge of the olive grove called Gethsemane, asking them to wait while he prays.

(b) Taking Peter, James and John with him, he goes on further saying to them 'The sorrow in my heart is so great that it almost crushes me. Stay here and keep watch.' (v.34 GNB). Death itself seems preferable.

(c) Going on alone he prays in anguish,
  - (i) 'Abba' — still the childlike attitude of trust in his father
  - (ii) that he might be spared 'this cup of suffering' but only
  - (iii) if it could be done in accordance with God's will.

TEST YOURSELF ON FACTS

1. Where did Jesus and his disciples go at the end of the last supper?
2. What did Jesus say would happen to the disciples?
3. What did Jesus say Peter would do?
4. Which disciples did Jesus take with him when he went to pray in the Garden of Gethsemane?
5. What did he pray to God?
6. What advice did he give the disciples? Why?
7. What did Jesus say to those sent to arrest him?
8. What false evidence was given against Jesus?
9. What was the first question the High Priest asked Jesus?
10. What was his second question?
11. What did Jesus reply?
12. Who was the first person to recognise him?
13. How did one of the bystanders recognise him?
14. How many times did they hear cockcrow?
15. How many times did Peter deny Jesus?

The Garden of Gethsemane on the Mount of Olives as it is today

(d) He returns to find Peter, James and John asleep and reproaches them — 'Weren't you able to stay awake even for one hour?' He reminds them of the necessity to pray since 'the spirit is willing but the flesh is weak.'
Try to imagine the sense of emptiness and loneliness in such a situation. Jesus must have felt as you would feel if your friends were to let you down badly at a difficult time when you particularly needed the comfort of knowing they were thinking about you.
(e) He returns to his private prayer, using the same words.
(f) When he comes back to the disciples they are once again asleep.
(g) He prays alone again.
(h) He returns to the disciples a third time saying 'Are you still sleeping?'

St Luke adds two extra details:
(i) Jesus was strengthened by an angel as he prayed.
(ii) His sweat was *like* drops of blood, so intense was his anguish.

3. THE ARREST

Mark 14.43 – 50: Matt. 26.47 – 56: Luke 22.47 – 53

Judas arrives with the Temple police. There are five things to notice in this part of the story:

(a) Judas betrays Jesus with a kiss. It has often been said that few things can be worse than using the sign of friendship as a signal of betrayal. However, we know that it was customary for pupils to greet their teacher with a kiss (times have changed!)
(b) Jesus points out that he poses no threat but is a teacher who has always taught openly.
(c) It is the Fourth Gospel which tells us that it was Peter who cut off the slave's ear and Luke who tells us that Jesus healed it (Notice that Luke does *not* say that Jesus picked up the ear and stuck it on. What do you think happened?)
(d) All these events happened in accordance with Old Testament prophecy.
(e) Only St Mark tells us of the young man who escaped. For his possible identity refer to Unit 1.2(a)(i).

4. TRIAL BEFORE THE HIGH PRIEST

Mark 14.53 – 65: Matt. 26.57 – 68: Luke 22.55, 63 – 71

The trial of Jesus falls into two parts:
(i) A religious trial before the Sanhedrin.
(ii) A political trial before the Roman governor.

Immediately after his arrest, Jesus is led before an informal meeting of the Sanhedrin under Caiaphas, the High Priest. Strictly speaking this is an illegal trial since formal meetings of the Sanhedrin could only be held between sunrise and sunset.

The charge is blasphemy — claiming to be the Messiah.

St Mark, followed by St Matthew, is uncompromising in saying that the Sanhedrin were trying to find evidence *against* Jesus in order to put him to death i.e. they knew the verdict they wanted, but that is not to say that the trial was unfairly conducted.

It took a long time to reach a verdict because, under Jewish Law (Deut. 19.15) evidence had to be supported by more than one witness and the witnesses did not agree.

The evidence referred to in Mark 14.57–59 when Jesus is reported to have said he would tear down the Temple and rebuild it in three days bears some relationship to something Jesus did say earlier in his ministry (Look up John 2.18–19) but, as this is a study of the Synoptic Gospels, there is no need to go into detail over this point. It is sufficient to know that the witnesses did not agree.

Learn accurately what happens next:

(a) The High Priest asks Jesus 'Have you no answer to the accusation they bring against you?'
(b) Jesus remains silent. He cannot deny the charge. He *is* the Messiah, but not the kind of Messiah the Jews are expecting. It would be useless to talk to them about the Suffering Servant in relation to the expected King of the Jews. (Unit 6.1). His silence fulfils what Isaiah had written about the Suffering Servant in Isa. 53.7.
(c) The High Priest asks 'Are you the Messiah?
(d) Jesus replies 'I AM' and continues with words from Dan. 7.13. I AM was regarded as the name of God (look up the story of Moses at the burning bush in Exod. 3.14) and would have been a shocking thing for a Jew to say — unless it were true.
(e) The High Priest tore his robes — his own, not Jesus' robes. This was a ritual action when a person was accused of blasphemy. In British Courts, in the days of the death penalty, the judge used to don a black cap before condemning a criminal to death.
(f) They all agreed he should be put to death.

This presented a problem. The Sanhedrin was not authorised to condemn a man to death. They needed the support of the Roman Governor but he would be unlikely to take notice of a charge of claiming to be Messiah. That would be regarded as a religious squabble among the Jews and certainly would not warrant the death penalty. The charge would therefore have to be 'adapted' to suit the Romans.

CHECK YOUR UNDERSTANDING

1. *What was the gallicinium?*
2. *Why was the midnight trial of Jesus illegal?*
3. *Explain the significance of Jesus' remaining silent when the High Priest asks him 'Have you no answer to the accusation?'*
4. *What is the significance of Jesus' quoting from the book of Daniel? (Look up Unit 6: The Messiah p.19).*
5. *What problem confronted the Sanhedrin in condemning Jesus to death?*

5. PETER'S DENIALS

Mark 14.66–72: Matt. 26.69–75: Luke 22.56–62

St Mark had said (14.50) that all the disciples had run away, yet here is Peter right inside the High Priest's courtyard, so all is not weakness and failure even though Peter must have felt his failure on this occasion very deeply. In fact we can be fairly sure that the account goes back to the apostle himself. At the time when Mark was writing nobody else would have wanted to show the leading apostle in such a damaging light. Learn accurately the order of the challenges:

(a) The serving maid recognises Peter and says, 'You, too, were with Jesus of Nazareth.'
(b) Peter denies it — 'I don't know . . . I don't understand what you are talking about'. But he moves into the shadows away from the fire where he might be recognised again.
(c) First cockcrow (i.e. bugle call).
(d) The servant girl points Peter out to others present — 'He is one of them.'
(e) Peter denies it a second time.
(f) One of the bystanders recognises his rough Galilean accent (as someone with an Irish accent might be at risk in a pub after an IRA explosion)
(g) Peter, really frightened now, swears an oath that he knows nothing about Jesus.
(h) Second cockcrow.
(i) Peter remembers what Jesus had said and breaks down and weeps.
(j) St Luke alone tells us that at just that moment Jesus is led away and that he turns and looks at Peter. Imagine the effect of that look (what kind of a look do you think it was?) on Peter.

WHAT DO YOU THINK?

Jesus could probably have escaped death up to the time of his arrest. Why did he choose *not* to escape? Can you see any connection between what happened in the Garden of Gethsemane and the Temptations at the outset of his ministry? (Unit 7)

Trial before Pilate. Herod

1. TRIAL BEFORE PILATE

Having decided that Jesus is guilty of blasphemy, the Jewish authorities have to go to the Roman Governor, Pontius Pilate, to obtain a death sentence.

> • *PILATE*
>
> *Pilate was governor of Judaea from* AD *26 – 36 and was also procurator i.e. responsible for procuring the necessary amount of tax. Josephus describes him as an 'inflexible, merciless and obstinate man continually given to corruption, violence and cruelty of every kind.' He seems to have shown no diplomacy in dealing with the Jews. On various occasions he acted in ways which would cause grave offence to their religious sensibilities and eventually he was removed from office and banished by the Emperor Caligula. The evangelists play down Pilate's responsibility for the death of Jesus. They are writing at a time when it was necessary to show that the Church posed no threat to the Roman Empire. So they suggest that it was the Jews rather than Pontius Pilate who bore responsibility for Jesus' death. Nevertheless succeeding generations only know of Pilate at all because of his part in the crucifixion of Jesus.*

The Romans used crucifixion as a way of putting wrongdoers to death and this suits the Sanhedrin particularly well. Jewish Law declares a hanged man to be cursed by God. If Jesus' body hangs on a cross, it will proclaim to everyone that God has rejected him and therefore he cannot possibly be the Messiah. However there is a difficulty. To a Roman, claiming to be Messiah would appear more in the nature of a religious squabble than a crime meriting a death sentence. The charge therefore has to be adapted to suit the occasion and we see in Pilate's first question, 'Are you the King of the Jews?' how this modification is achieved. To the Jews the Messiah would be their king, but to the Romans claiming to be king posed a political threat to the government which Pilate is bound to take seriously. Notice the three charges listed by St Luke (23.1)

(a) Subverting the nation
(b) Opposing the payment of taxes to Caesar
(c) Claiming to be Messiah, a king.

As in the case of the trial before the Sanhedrin, learn carefully and accurately the sequence of events:

(a) Pilate asks 'Are you the King of the Jews?'
(b) Jesus replies 'The words are yours' (i.e. he can neither affirm nor deny it. He *is* the king of the Jews, but not the kind they are expecting.)
(c) Pilate asks 'Have you nothing to say in your defence?'
(d) Jesus remains silent. (Remember the prophecy in Isaiah 53.7 Unit 27.4(b)).

2. HEROD Luke 23.6 – 12

St Luke alone tells us of the hearing before Herod. Strictly speaking this is not a trial. Learning that Jesus comes from Galilee, Pilate sends him to Herod Antipas, ruler of the area, for a report. If Jesus is a known troublemaker, Herod would be aware of it.

> **THE HEROD FAMILY**
>
> **King Herod the Great ruled Palestine under the Roman Emperor until his death in 4 BC.**
>
> **When he died the area he had governed was divided between his sons. One of them, Herod Antipas, had expected to inherit everything from his father and was furious to find his father had changed his will. It was left to the Emperor Augustus to settle the quarrel between the brothers. Eventually the territory was divided as follows:**
>
> **Archelaus was made ruler of Judaea, Samaria and Idumaea.**
>
> **Herod Antipas was made ruler of Galilee and Peraea.**
>
> **Philip was made ruler of the area at the foot of Mt. Hermon.**
>
> **All three brothers were unpopular with their subjects. Archelaus upset the Jews so much that they appealed to the Roman Emperor who banished him. His territory was then put into the hands of a Roman governor. At the time of Jesus' death this governor was Pontius Pilate.**

TEST YOURSELF ON FACTS
1. Who took Jesus to Pilate?
2. What were Pilate's first words to Jesus?
3. What did Jesus reply?
4. How did Jesus respond to Pilate's next question?
5. Who was Barabbas?
6. Why was Herod pleased to see Jesus?
7. How did Jesus behave towards Herod?
8. How did Herod treat Jesus?

Jesus had earlier referred to Herod as 'that fox' (Luke 13.32), a fair indication of his character. Jesus refuses to entertain him by performing miracles so is treated with contempt and returned to Pilate dressed as a mock king. Mark and Matthew tell us this mockery was carried out by the Roman guard. We do not know the reason for the earlier quarrel between Pilate and Herod which is healed by this episode.

3. JESUS IS CONDEMNED TO DEATH

The evangelists, preaching in a world dominated by Rome, are at pains to show that the Roman governor himself realises that Jesus is innocent. He tries to release him through a Passover custom of freeing one prisoner. The crowd however shout for Barabbas (= 'son of the father'). He, almost certainly, had been involved in rebellion against Rome and so was a popular freedom fighter whereas Jesus had merely disappointed any Messianic expectation the crowd might have had of him. In the end Pilate gives way to the crowd and condemns a man he knows to be innocent.

Jesus is scourged (v.15), a terrible punishment which was the normal prelude to crucifixion. The prisoner was so weakened by whipping that it shortened the period he was hanging alive on the cross.

St Mark, followed by St Matthew, tells us of further mockery by the soldiers who dressed Jesus in a soldier's cloak to represent the cloak of the Emperor and hammered thorny branches around his brow to represent the Emperor's spiky crown. They then went through a parody of the shouts of 'Ave Caesar' with which the Roman Emperor was greeted, beat him, spat on him and fell on their knees in mock homage.

At the end of it all, Jesus is led away to be crucified.

4. ADDITIONS IN ST MATTHEW'S GOSPEL

Three examples of material found only in Matthew need to be noticed:

(a) The death of Judas (Matt. 27.3–9)
St Matthew tells us that, after his betrayal, Judas was filled with remorse and, having thrown the money back at the High Priest, went and hanged himself. (If you want to read a conflicting account of Judas' end, look at Acts 1.18 where he spends his reward on a field only to fall to his death there).

(b) Pilate's wife's dream (Matt. 27.19)

(c) Pilate washes his hands (Matt. 27.24)
Matthew implies that Pilate performs this as a symbolic action to show that he is not responsible for the death of Jesus. In fact such an action would be typical of Jews (Deut. 21.6–7) rather than of Romans.

CHECK YOUR UNDERSTANDING
1. *Explain how the charge of 'blasphemy' was modified to suit a trial before the Roman governor.*
2. *Can you suggest a reason for Jesus' replying to Pilate, 'the words are yours'?*
3. *Can you suggest reasons why the crowd preferred Barabbas to Jesus?*
4. *Why was Jesus sent to Herod?*
5. *Explain the significance of the soldiers' mockery of Jesus.*

WHAT DO YOU THINK?
1. Do you think it was right to adapt the charge brought against Jesus to suit the Roman governor i.e. to play political games with a man's life?
2. What does it tell us about Pontius Pilate that he would condemn a man he knew to be innocent?

Way of the Cross. Crucifixion. Burial.

Mark 15.21 – 47: Matt. 27.34 – 61: Luke 23.26 – 56

1. WAY OF THE CROSS

The sentence of crucifixion once passed had to be carried out. Should the prisoner die on the way to the place of execution the soldier guarding him was crucified instead. This rough and ready arrangement prevented excessive ill-treatment of prisoners.

Be careful to learn the sequence of events accurately and in detail.

The prisoner carried the crossbeam (Latin *patibulum*) of his own cross. The uprights were left in position to be used again. As Jesus fell under the weight of the cross, a soldier used his power to order Simon, a visitor from Cyrene in North Africa, to carry the cross for him (cf. Unit 18.4 (d)). St Mark adds the detail of the names of Simon's two sons without comment. Clearly they were sufficiently well-known in the early Christian community to count as reliable witnesses of the events being described.

Golgotha (v.22) is the Aramaic name, Calvary its Latin version. The site was probably a hill outside Jerusalem, possibly skull-shaped as a result of quarrying.

Prisoners were given drugged wine to help deaden the pain. Its provision was one of the charitable works of the women of Jerusalem, but St Mark tells us Jesus refused it.

2. THE CRUCIFIXION

The evangelists show remarkable restraint in their accounts of the crucifixion. It was a horrifying way of dying which their readers would know all about. Death from exhaustion and gradual suffocation might take days.

Soldiers guarding the condemned prisoners during this time were allowed the keep the victims' clothing — small compensation for an unpleasant duty — but on this occasion the evangelists see this practice as the fulfilment of Psalm 22.18.

The whole of the crucifixion story needs to be read with this psalm in mind. *Look it up and read it carefully*. Jesus would have known the psalms and prayed them day by day. It seems probable he was praying this particular psalm as he hung on the cross and the evangelists record several echoes from it in what happened.

Christ of St John of the Cross, painting by Salvador Dali

Above his head was fixed the titulus (Mark verse 26) recording the charge. This was done as a warning to others. Its wording, naming Jesus king of the Jews, was so important to the early Christians that it is one of the few details which appears in all four gospels, although each

> **INRI**
> **The letters INRI which are often shown on a crucifix stand for Iesus Nazarenus Rex Iudaeorum i.e. Jesus of Nazareth, King of the Jews.**

evangelist expresses it in slightly different words. They wished to emphasise that, despite all evidence to the contrary, Jesus died as the Messiah.

The mocking which is recorded next (Mark 15.29–32) is designed to convey the hostility of the Jewish people. Remember the evangelists were writing for people living under Roman rule and it would have been undiplomatic to lay all the blame for the crucifixion on the Roman governor who passed the sentence. This mockery is another form of the temptation to prove himself to be Messiah by miraculous means (cf. Unit 7).

From noon until 3 p.m. a strange darkness covered the country (v.33). Here the symbolism is of greater importance than what actually happened. It could not have been an eclipse of the sun since that is physically impossible when the moon is full, as it must always be at Passover. Some scholars have suggested there may have been a black sirocco but what matters most is the gospels' convicton that the powers of darkness seem to be supreme as Jesus is dying on the cross.

Then Jesus cries out from the cross. *Learn the Aramaic words as well as their meaning*. They are in fact the opening words of Psalm 22. This great cry of dereliction (= being abandoned) from the cross can be interpreted in two ways:

(a) As a cry of loss. Jesus is now so totally identified with mankind at its worst that for a time he too experiences a break in his communion with God.

(b) As a prayer of trust. Read Psalm 22 again to the very end. You will see how its mood changes and that, by the end, the psalmist reaffirms his trust in God whatever happens.

The reference to Elijah (v.35) arises from a confusion with the Aramaic word 'Eloi'. Elijah was believed to come to the aid of good people in trouble.

Additions in St Luke's Gospel

(a) Women of Jerusalem (Luke 23.27–31)

The women set up the wailing usually reserved for mourning after death. Jesus' words are sometimes regarded as a prediction of the fall of Jerusalem in AD 70.

(b) The penitent thief (Luke 23.39–43)

One of the criminals crucified with Jesus reviles him, the other repents and asks Jesus to remember him. He then receives a promise of Paradise (a Persian word meaning a formal garden which is also used of the Garden of Eden in Genesis 1–3).

(c) Three additional 'Words from the cross'
Learn these carefully.

(i) As he is nailed to the cross, 'Forgive them,

'Student Cross' on pilgrimage to Walsingham in Holy Week

Father! They don't know what they are doing.' (23.34 GNB)

(ii) to the penitent thief, 'I promise you that today you will be in Paradise with me.' (23.43 GNB)

(iii) 'Father! In your hands I place my spirit!' (23.46 GNB) — words of trust and submission to God's will but also a quotation from Psalm 31.5.

All three gospels tell us of the tearing of the curtain in the Temple. This curtain was in front of the Holy of Holies where only the High Priest was allowed to enter (Unit 24. p73). It thus represented a barrier between God and Man which Christians believe to have been removed by Christ's sacrifice on the cross.

In Greek the words of the centurion (Mark 15.39) could mean *either* 'Truly this man was *a* son of God' *or 'the* Son of God.' The Christian faith naturally favours the latter translation.

3. THE BURIAL

Jewish Law (Deut. 21.23) required the bodies of criminals to be buried the same day. Jesus died at three o'clock on Friday afternoon and the sabbath, on which no work could be done, began at sunset. So time was short. Joseph of Arimathea asked Pilate for permission to take the body. It was a brave action openly to show concern for the body of someone condemned for treason. St Mark tells us that Joseph was a member of the Sanhedrin but that he had not been associated with the condemnation of Jesus. Having ascertained that Jesus was dead, Pilate gave permission for the removal of the body and Joseph then wrapped it in a linen cloth and buried it in a rock tomb, rolling a stone across the entrance. Only St Matthew tells us the tomb belonged to Joseph himself. Luke and John tell us it had never been used before. All three gosepls tell us that women saw where the body was laid. it will become apparent later why it was important that they should have been quite sure in which tomb Jesus was buried.

Additions in St Matthew's Gospel

There are a number of additions in St Matthew's Gospel which heighten the remarkable nature of what happened. They seem to have been made to emphasise the Christian beliefs about Jesus.

(a) There was an earthquake as Jesus died and the bodies of 'the saints' came out of their tombs (27.51–53)
St Matthew is expressing the Christian faith that Jesus is the Resurrection and the Life (John 11.25) and that through him the way to eternal life has been opened up for all mankind.

(b) The tomb was sealed and a guard placed on it (27.62–66). The religious authorities feared the disciples might steal the body and then claim Jesus had risen from the dead. Pilate granted permission for the tomb to be guarded — a fact which will slightly change St Matthew's account of the resurrection.

TEST YOURSELF ON FACTS

1. Who carried the cross of Jesus? Can you name his two sons?
2. What is the name of the place where Jesus was crucified?
3. What did the soldiers do after nailing Jesus to the cross?
4. What time was Jesus crucified?
5. What did the titulus say?
6. Who else was crucified with him?
7. What did the jeering crowds say?
8. What did the chief priests and scribes say?
9. What happened at noon?
10. What did Jesus cry out at 3 o'clock? What did people think he said?
11. What additional sayings from the cross does St Luke tell us?
12. What happened in the Temple when Jesus died?
13. What did the centurion guarding the cross say?
14. Who asked Pilate for the body of Jesus?
15. What did he do with Jesus' body?

CHECK YOUR UNDERSTANDING

1. *What was the significance of:*
   (a) the darkness
   (b) the tearing of the curtain in the Temple when Jesus died?
2. *Read Psalm 22. What connections can you see with the story of the death of Jesus?*
3. *Write short comments on each of the sayings from the cross.*
4. *Look again at the characteristics of St Matthew's Gospel in Unit 1 (c) (iii). In what ways is his account of the crucifixion and burial of Jesus characteristic of him?*

WHAT DO YOU THINK?
If God is all-powerful and all-loving why did he allow Jesus to die in such a horrible way?

Resurrection. Ascension

The last chapter of each gospel tells us about the Resurrection. Of this central doctrine of the Christian faith St Paul was to write 'if Christ has not been raised, then your faith is a delusion' (1 Corinth.15.17 GNB), so it is probably true to say that, over the years, no event has been accorded so much critical attention or provoked so many arguments. For GCSE you are not required to grapple with all the arguments but rather to study in detail what the gospels tell us remembering that they are the faith documents of the Church. Inevitably you are then likely to be stimulated to explore further the question of the profound and decisive effect the resurrection has had on Christians in every generation. But the first and most important step, as we said right at the beginning of this book, is to STUDY THE TEXT.
Resurrection stories fall into two groups — those concerning the empty tomb and those concerning appearances of the risen Christ to his friends.

1. THE EMPTY TOMB

(a) MARK 16.1–8

Nothing could be done till after the Sabbath. Then Mary Magdalene, Mary the mother of James, and Salome (the mother of the Zebedee brothers) go to anoint the body. These three women had been present at the crucifixion and had seen where the body was buried. The implication is that they did not go to the wrong tomb by mistake.
Anointing the body was part of the normal Jewish burial practice. There had been no time to do this before the hasty burial on the Friday afternoon, but the anointing at Bethany (Unit 25.7) then takes on a new significance.
Having set off at the crack of dawn, the women wonder how they are to get into the tomb since the stone closing the entrance is too heavy for them to move.
Finding the stone has been rolled back, they see 'a young man wearing a white robe' — an angel (N.B. *one* angel in Mark and Matthew, *two* angels in Luke and John. Lessing makes the delightful comment, 'do ye not see then that the evangelists do not count the angels? There were not only two angels, there were millions of them.') The presence of angels signifies that God is involved with this empty tomb.
The women are dumbfounded and the angel speaks to reassure them (compare the angel's first words to Zechariah, Mary and the shepherds). He gives them a message for the disciples, singling out Peter (remember Mark's connection with Peter and the fact that Peter had denied his master). Jesus will go before them into Galilee (like a shepherd leading his flock). The women run away terrified and say nothing to anyone. At this point the authentic part of St Mark's Gospel ends. What follows (16.9–20) is known as 'the longer ending' and is a second century addition which summarises the appearances of the risen Christ. Scholars are

St John's Cross, Iona

divided as to whether Mark intended to end his Gospel at verse 8. It is possible he was interrupted (remember he was writing during the Neronian persecution) or possibly the outside of the manuscript containing his own conclusion was lost. For the examination you need not study beyond verse 8.

(b) MATTHEW 28.1 – 8

St Matthew follows St Mark's account but notice the differences:

(i) Only the two Marys are mentioned as going to the tomb.

(ii) He does not mention that the women were concerned about moving the stone since he has told us the tomb has been sealed and a guard placed upon it (27.66). He therefore says the women had gone 'to look at the tomb'.

(iii) Matthew alone attempts to describe the resurrection, speaking of an earthquake. He tells us the guards 'trembled and became like dead men' as the stone was rolled away by an angel.

(iv) The women leave the tomb *with joy* to take the angel's message to the disciples.

CHECK YOUR UNDERSTANDING

1. *Why did the women have to wait till Sunday morning before going to the tomb?*
2. *Why is it important that the evangelists have named the women who went to the tomb?*
3. *Give two possible reasons for the abrupt ending of St Mark's Gospel at verse 8.*
4. *Look up 1 Corinth. 15.3 – 8 and list the people to whom Jesus appeared according to St Paul. Which of these appearances are mentioned in the Synoptic Gospels?*
5. *How many references can you find which emphasise that Jesus was present in body after the resurrection?*
6. *Why was it important that the apostles were witnesses of the post-resurrection appearances of Jesus?*

TEST YOURSELF ON FACTS

1. What do we call the day that Jesus rose from the dead?
2. Why did the women go to the tomb according to (a) Mark (b) Matthew?
3. What did they see when they reached the tomb?
4. What instructions does the angel give the women?
5. What do the women do then according to (a) Mark (b) Luke?
6. According to Matthew, what were the guard told when they reported the resurrection to the Sanhedrin?
7. According to St Matthew what instructions does Jesus give his disciples before leaving them?
8. What are the last words of St Matthew's Gospel?
9. Where were Cleopas and his companion going when they were joined by Jesus?
10. In what two ways did they come to recognise Jesus?
11. What had they felt as he spoke to them on the road?
12. When the two disciples returned to Jerusalem they found someone else had seen Jesus. Who was it?
13. They were to wait before going out to preach. What for?
14. What emotion, characteristic of Luke's Gospel, did the disciples feel as they returned to Jerusalem?

(c) LUKE 24.1 – 12

St Luke tells us there were two angels at the tomb. They tell the women Jesus has been raised and remind them that Jesus himself had predicted as much. They do not send a message to the disciples but the women return and tell the disciples what they have found (*why only eleven disciples?*)
Someone called Joanna, not named by Matthew and Mark, is included among the women at the tomb.
The disciples do not believe the women's story (and a woman's evidence did not count in a court of law) so Peter himself goes to investigate and finds the women have been telling the truth.

EASTER
Christians celebrate the resurrection on Easter Sunday. The word 'Easter' comes from the name of a pagan goddess, Eostre, whose festival was kept in the spring. Easter Sunday is a moveable feast, being kept on the first Sunday after full moon on or after 21st March.

2. APPEARANCES TO HIS FRIENDS

(a) 1 CORINTH. 15.3 – 8

Although strictly speaking not part of your syllabus, you should know that the earliest reference to the resurrection occurs in a letter St Paul wrote to Christians in Corinth (see introduction 1(b)(i)). St Paul mentions six occasions on which Jesus appeared after the resurrection. Three of these appearances are described in the gospels.

b) MATTHEW 28.9 AND 28.16 – 20

(i) The first appearance recorded by St Matthew occurs as the women leave the empty tomb 'afraid and yet filled with joy'. Jesus meets them. Notice his first words to them, 'Peace be with you.' They are to be repeated on later occasions. Jesus then reiterates the message of the angel and the women take hold of his feet and worship him (Remember worship is characteristic of this Gospel).

Matthew then gives us information special to his Gospel. The soldiers go to report what has happened to the Sanhedrin and are bribed to say that the disciples have stolen the body.

(ii) The second appearance described by St Matthew occurs on a hill top in Galilee. Remember the significance of hilltop experiences — the Transfiguration, the giving of the New Law in the Sermon on the Mount and now Christ's final departure from them. Notice the details:

- Eleven disciples went to the hill.
- They worshipped him, though some doubted.
- Jesus gives them their final instructions saying:
  - All authority belongs to him.
  - They are to go to all nations to make them disciples.
  - They are to baptize in the name of the Holy Trinity.
  - They are to teach people to obey Christ's commands.

Most important of all, he himself will be forever with them. His disciples need not fear. Although his physical presence must leave them, his followers can be certain that his spirit will be forever available to them.

(c) LUKE 24.13 – 53

(i) The road to Emmaus 24.13 – 35

This story appears only in St Luke's Gospel.

Two disciples (i.e. followers of Jesus — they were not numbered among the Twelve) are walking home from Jerusalem to Emmaus. One of them is called Cleopas. The other may well have been his wife (she can be said to be Mary's sister.) As they walk they are joined by another traveller. It would have been a normal safety precaution to join other travellers on a lonely road. Notice that the two are not struck by anything unusual in the man who joins them. There is no suggestion that they are seeing a ghost. Their only surprise is at his apparent ignorance of the events in Jerusalem which are in the forefront of their own minds and which they describe to him. He replies (*learn his actual words as far as possible*) by referring to scripture and explaining to them the prophecies about himself which concerned the events they are discussing. As they come to Emmaus they invite the stranger to stay with them and then, in the breaking of bread, recognise Jesus and he vanishes. It is then that they remember how their hearts 'had burned within them' as they spoke to him on the road (fire is a symbol of the presence of God).

Interesting as it may be to speculate on ways in which they might have recognised him (e.g. by the scars of the crucifixion), to Christians the main point of the story lies in the fact that Cleopas and his companion recognised Jesus in two ways — through scripture and in the breaking of bread. Since these are the ways in which Christians in every generation come to know Christ — through scripture and in Holy Communion — this first post-resurrection recognition in these two ways is important. They are so excited they turn round and walk all the way back to Jerusalem — making a round trip of perhaps fifteen miles in the dark, such was their sense of urgency — only to find that others have also seen the risen Lord, *including Peter*. Although this appearance to Peter is not described in the gospels, the fact that it occurred is borne out by 1 Corinth. 15.5.

(ii) Appearance to the Twelve 24.36 – 49

While they are talking, suddenly Jesus is there among them. This time they are terrified, thinking they are seeing a ghost. Notice Christ's greeting — 'Peace be with you.'

On this occasion Luke goes out of his way to emphasise that Jesus is not a ghost. Jesus invites them to touch him and, when they are still incredulous, asks them for supper and shares a meal of cooked fish with them. The implication is that ghosts do not eat fish!

Again he explains the writings about himself in scripture (i.e. the Old Testament prophecies). Pay careful attention to his instructions to the disciples:

- They are witnesses. Later (Acts 1.21), when the disciples had to choose someone to join their number to replace Judas Iscariot, the chief qualification they were seeking was that the chosen person should personally have seen the risen Christ. Remember that, earlier in his ministry, Jesus did not send out the Twelve until they had *been with* him. The gospel is transmitted through personal experience, not hearsay.
- They are to go out and, starting in Jerusalem, are to preach the message about repentance and forgiveness to all nations.
- They are to do so in his name and through the power which will be given to them by God.

(iii) The final parting 24.50–53

The story of the Ascension is to be expanded by St Luke in the Acts of the Apostles (Act 1.6–11). Here he merely tells us that Jesus led them out as far as Bethany and, as he blessed them, he was taken up into heaven. There had to be a moment of definite parting if the disciples were to obey Jesus and go out and preach. Bearing in mind the first century belief in a three-tier universe (with heaven above and hell beneath the earth) Jesus went *up* to show them clearly where he was going. In the Acts of the Apostles, Luke tells us a cloud received him — that cloud (the *shekinah*) which shows the presence of God. Again the disciples *worshipped* him and Luke then concludes his Gospel where he had begun it — in the Temple where the disciples in *great joy* thank God for all he has given them in Christ.

So ends our study of the Synoptic Gospels. Central to them is the person of Jesus of Nazareth whom Christians believe to be the Christ. These gospels were the earliest attempt to show how the first Christians came to this belief. Yet, in the concluding words of the Fourth Gospel, 'there are many other things that Jesus did. If they were all written down one by one, I suppose that the whole world could not hold the books that would be written.' (GNB)

● *TWENTIETH CENTURY VIEWS*

Twentieth century theologians have offered new interpretations of the resurrection. You are not required to grapple with these for GCSE, although your teacher may wish to discuss some of them with you. If you intend pursuing your study beyond this level, you will at once be faced with the problems raised. The best preparation for such a study is a thorough knowledge of the text. That is the foundation of any objective study of Jesus and that is what this book has aimed to provide.

WHAT DO YOU THINK?

1. What replies would you make to people who made the following suggestions to explain the resurrection?
   The women went to the wrong tomb.
   The body was stolen by the disciples.
   The body was not really dead, revived and escaped.
   It was 'all psychological' and wishful thinking on the part of the disciples.
2. What difference does it make whether Jesus rose from the dead or not?

INDEX

(Bold figures indicate main reference)

ACKNOWLEDGEMENTS
Front Cover photographs: St John's Cross, Iona (Bill Meadows); An estate, Bicester (Andrew McKnight); Crib, St Barnabas, Ealing (The Revd Preb. R. N. Hetherington); Salisbury Cathedral (Ivan J. Belcher); School girls (Mrs Denise Sims); Garden of Gethsemane (John Baggley); Residents in Old People's Home (Andrew McKnight); Container depot, Cardiff (Paul Felix); A Baptism (Andrew McKnight); Boys of the Kent County Youth Orchestra playing football (Clare Morgan).

Photographs on text pages are reproduced by kind permission of: BBC Hulton Picture Library (pp.30, 47); The Revd John Baggley (p.21); Kenneth Baker (pp.55, 81); Barnarby's Picture Library (pp.5, 38, 58 both, 64); The Billy Graham Evangelistic Association Ltd (p.4); Camera Press (p.59); M. F. Couchman Esq (p.34); The Revd Michael Day (p.67); Robert Deeley (p.53); Keith Ellis (pp.19, 69); Glasgow Art Gallery and Museum (p.88); The Guide Dogs for the Blind Association (p.65); Sonia Halliday (p.39); Harris Morgan & Son, and Nash's Bakery, Bicester (p.51); Harrison/Parrott Ltd (p.52); H.M. Customs and Excise (p.25); The Revd Prebendary R. N. Hetherington (p.16); Frank Hoskins (p.89); Judges Postcards, and St Leonard's Church (p.49); London Zoo (pp.62, 71); Dennis Mansell (p.32); Stephen Mayes (p.2); Bill Meadows (p.91); The Revd C. Paxton (p.83); The Revd Donald Pharaoh (p.24); Popperfoto (pp.18, 48); W. Russell Read (p.12); Ronald Sheridan's Photo Library (pp.45, 78); The Revd Christopher Rowley (pp.84, 94); The Revd Mark Sumner (p.29); Graham Tatlock (p.23); USPG (p.28).

Line illustrations are reproduced by kind permission of Board of Deputies of British Jews (p.36); the Central Board of Finance of the Church of England from *Lent, Holy Week, Easter,* published by Church House Publishing, Cambridge University Press and SPCK (1986) (pp.5, 6, 7); Jackie Edwards (p.60); Mabel Hayes, from Teaching Christianity Resource Book published by Mowbray (p.73); Ian Norman, adapted from *A Pocket Guide for Servers* published by Mowbray (p.10); Sr Elizabeth Ruth, ODC (pp.4, 8).

The author and publisher are grateful to the following for permission to reproduce extracts from copyright works: *Good News Bible* © American Bible Society 1966, 1971, 1976, published by The Bible Societies and Collins; *New English Bible,* Second Edition © 1970 by permission of Oxford and Cambridge University Presses. Extracts from the Authorized King James Version of the Bible, which is Crown Copyright in the United Kingdom, are reproduced by permission of Eyre & Spottiswoode (Publisher) Limited, Her Majesty's Printers, London. The extract from Baptism and Confirmation in *The Alternative Service Book 1980* is reproduced with permission. The Scripture quotations contained herein (RSV) are from the *Revised Standard Version* of the Bible, copyrighted 1946, 1952, 1971 by the Division of Christian Education of the National Council of the Churches of Christ in the USA, and are used by permission. All rights reserved.

I wish to thank the following for their help: Mr Edwin Cox whose sympathetic understanding and wide experience have been invaluable; Miss Brenda Harrison for helpful comments on the illustrations; The Revd M. Eyden and the Revd M. Fletcher who read and commented on parts of the manuscript in the light of their own classroom experience; Mr. Kenneth Baker, Managing Director, Publishing of A.R. Mowbray & Co Ltd, for his encouragement and patience without which the book might never have been finished.

If the author has unwittingly transgressed any copyright, she makes sincere apologies and will acknowledge any such oversights in future editions.
3 February 1987 D.M.